Child Abuse

Child Abuse

A Handbook for Health Care Practitioners

Ivan Blumenthal MRCP DCh

Consultant Paediatrician, Royal Oldham Hospital,
Oldham, UK

Edward Arnold
A member of the Hodder Headline Group
LONDON   NEW YORK   MELBOURNE   AUCKLAND

© 1994 IVAN BLUMENTHAL

First published in Great Britain 1994

British Library Cataloguing in Publication Data

Blumenthal, Ivan
  Child Abuse: Handbook for Health Care
  Practitioners
  I. Title
  362.76

  ISBN 0–340–60141–8

Whilst the advice and information in this book is believed to be true
and accurate at the date of going to press, neither the author nor the
publisher can accept any legal responsibility or liability for any errors
or omissions that may be made. In particular (but without limiting
the generality of the preceding disclaimer) every effort has been made
to check drug dosages; however, it is still possible that errors have
been missed. Furthermore, dosage schedules are constantly being
revised and new side effects recognised. For these reasons the reader
is strongly urged to consult the drug companies' printed instructions
before administering any of the drugs recommended in this book.

Typeset in 10/12 pt Times by Anneset, Weston-super-Mare, Avon.
Printed and bound in Great Britain for Edward Arnold, a division
of Hodder Headline PLC, 338 Euston Road, London NW1 3BH by
J. W. Arrowsmith Ltd, Bristol.

Contents

Preface

As a medical student in the late 1960s I cannot remember a single lecture on child abuse in the undergraduate curriculum. Such an omission is perhaps not surprising considering that C Henry Kempe and colleagues only coined the term 'battered child syndrome' in 1962. Nowadays all medical students receive instruction on child abuse. However, owing to the competing needs of the undergraduate curriculum relatively little time is devoted to such an important subject. Some formal postgraduate training is available, but minimal emphasis is given to it in postgraduate examinations. In general most child abuse education continues to be self-taught, expertise being acquired in practice. Increased media attention together with this autodidactic approach has created an even stronger need for a reliable source of reference for the doctor of today.

There are many British books which focus on the social and other specific effects of child abuse but few which cover all the medical aspects comprehensively. To meet this need I have written *Child Abuse* primarily for medical practitioners whose work brings them into regular contact with children. The aim of the book is to provide a concise reference which will not only aid diagnosis, but will also contain information about current child abuse procedures and English law. It should be noted that the law is not uniform throughout the United Kingdom. Readers in other parts of Britain and elsewhere will need to consult the law in their locality. Additional information that is not in the text can be obtained from the Further Reading references at the end of each section. In view of the controversy surrounding sexual abuse, that section has been referenced more extensively.

This book would be of particular use to medical students, paediatric nurses and health visitors. I have tried to minimise medical jargon so that it would appeal to non medical professionals such as social workers, psychologists, solicitors and the police who may require medical information as part of their work.

In the United Kingdom in the 1980s there were a number of child abuse Inquiries leading up to the Children Act 1989. The overriding message emanating from those Inquiries and enshrined in the Act is that the interest of the child is paramount and that interest is best served by close co-operation between the professions. This philosophy has been incorporated in *Child Abuse*.

Ivan Blumenthal
April 1993

Acknowledgements

I would like to express my gratitude to Jennifer Holden for typing the manuscript and its many drafts. In writing this book I have received much librarial assistance. I thank Margaret Kenway and Pam O'Neil of the Postgraduate Medical Centre, and Barbara Brierley of the Nursing Library, Oldham. Lastly, but not least, I thank my wife Liz and sons Morris and Toby. Their support and encouragement has been invaluable.

Note at proof stage to page 10

In June 1994 the Department of Health published the most extensive scientific survey of ritual abuse in the United Kingdom. The research was undertaken over two years by Professor Jean La Fontaine. She studied 84 cases and found no evidence of satanic abuse. In three cases sexual abusers claimed to have mystical powers as a strategy to entrap children and keep them from disclosing. In those cases the purpose was sexual and the ritual incidental to it. Professor La Fontaine concluded; 'Cases of satanic abuse are not a large-scale problem. They represent a minute proportion of child protection work'.

1 The epidemiology of child abuse

The young are weak, dependent and defenceless, making them vulnerable to abuse and exploitation. Child abuse has existed for centuries with tacit acceptance by society. The lot of children is vividly portrayed in literary works, most notably those of Dickens, Victor Hugo, Hardy and Brothers Grimm. It is ironic that the first court case for the protection of a child was instigated by the American Society for the Prevention of Cruelty to Animals in 1874 on the grounds that the child was part of the animal kingdom. In Britain the first charter for the protection of children (National Society for the Prevention of Cruelty to Children) appeared in 1889, some 67 years after the introduction of legislation to protect animals. The plight of British children during the Industrial Revolution is legend. While pioneers such as Lord Shaftesbury set out to protect children at work there was little urge to protect children from the evils of the domestic environment. The current high profile enjoyed by child protection agencies owes much to the seminal work of C Henry Kempe, a paediatrician in Denver, USA. First reports of x-ray evidence of abuse appeared in the 1940s and 1950s, but received little attention. The subject rose to prominence in 1962 when Kempe published his classic paper in the *Journal of the American Medical Association* in which he coined the term 'the battered child syndrome'. Largely through the effort of Kempe and his colleagues the plight of abused children became increasingly recognised.

In Britain two orthopaedic surgeons, Griffiths and Moynihan, first drew attention to the 'Battered Baby Syndrome' in a report in the *British Medical Journal* in December 1963. Their report together with a leading article in the same issue was very influential in bringing child abuse to the attention of the medical community. Awareness of the condition was given impetus by reports from forensic pathologists, notably Professor Keith Simpson, and paediatricians. The British Paediatric Association published a memorandum in the *British Medical Journal* in 1966 on the recognition and management of the problem. Previous reports, mainly by forensic pathologists, had seen this problem as primarily a police matter. The British Paediatric Association memorandum was a watershed in that for the first time emphasis was given to child abuse being a problem for 'medical' and 'social welfare' agencies. The monograph stated that if abuse was suspected 'the proper person to consult at this stage is the Children's Officer of the Local Authority'. In 1968 the NSPCC Battered Child Research Unit was formed under the leadership of a psychiatric social worker, Joan Court. She and her staff gave further publicity to child abuse by a large number of publications in a variety of journals.

In terms of media attention 1973 was a landmark. Until then the media had shown little interest in the subject. In January 1973 Maria Collwell died as a consequence of child abuse. In May of the same year a multidisciplinary meeting to discuss child abuse was convened in Tunbridge Wells under the chairmanship of an eminent paediatrician, Alfred White Franklin. This meeting was attended by Sir Keith Joseph, Secretary of State, and senior civil servants from the Department of Health and Social Security. Six days after the conference Sir Keith announced an Inquiry into the death of Maria Collwell. The subsequent Inquiry which was held at the end of the year was the turning point. Media interest became intense. A blow by blow account of the Inquiry was presented, often with sensational headlines. The net effect was to prick the conscience of the nation.

Since Maria Collwell there have been more than 30 Public Inquiries into the death of abused children. Names such as Jasmine Beckford, Kimberley Carlile, Tyra Henry have at times become household names. Many of these Inquiries were critical of social workers for having done too little too late. The recommendations of these Inquiries were heeded; as a consequence child abuse procedures developed from their inchoate state in the 1970s to the formal structure of the 1990s. The basic tenet pervading such procedures is the close co-operation between professionals.

In the late 1970s in the USA David Finkelhor, a psychologist, while working with the victims of child sexual abuse, became aware of the frequency of this type of abuse. His research was given prominence and succeeded in bringing child sexual abuse to the forefront of the child maltreatment problem. In Britain in the 1980s such research was given impetus by very vivid accounts of child sexual abuse by two enthusiastic paediatricians, Hobbs and Wynne. They published a number of reports of child sexual abuse in the *Lancet* and other distinguished journals. Influenced by the work of Hobbs and Wynne two paediatricians at Middlesbrough General Hospital, Cleveland, in 1987 diagnosed child sexual abuse in large numbers of children over a very short period. Children were taken into care causing much family disruption and distress. This 'epidemic' of child sexual abuse soon became public knowledge. The frenetic media attention given to it soon provoked a public outcry. To assuage public anxiety an Inquiry was convened under the Chairmanship of Justice Butler-Sloss. In contrast to other Inquiries the Cleveland Inquiry revealed that social workers and other professionals had been overzealous. The Cleveland Inquiry received widespread publicity and there were many lessons to be learned from it. It also served to highlight the parlous state of the law as it related to child protection. At about the same time as the Cleveland Inquiry a change in child care law was being mooted. Following the Inquiry the resolve for such change became irresistible, culminating in the Children Act 1989. The overriding principle of the Act is that the welfare of the child is paramount.

Types of abuse

For ease of classification abuse is generally categorised as physical, sexual, emotional and neglect. These types are not mutually exclusive. For example many children who are sexually abused are also physically abused.

1. Physical abuse (also called non-accidental injury)

Physical punishment is still commonplace in society. Abuse is deemed to have occurred when the degree or type of punishment would be unacceptable to society at large. Kempe said 'child abuse is the difference between a hand on the bottom and a fist in the face'. Punishment appropriate for the age of the child is a further consideration. A spank on the bottom would be unacceptable in a three month old, but could be condoned in a naughty three year old.

Physical abuse includes poisoning, burning, kicking, biting, throwing and shaking of children. Striking a child with a fist or an instrument is abuse. Physical discipline should not be used on children in infancy.

2. Sexual abuse

The National Centre for Child Abuse and Neglect in the USA defines sexual abuse as follows: 'Sexual abuse consists of contacts or interactions between a child and an adult when the child is being used for sexual stimulation of the adult or another person. Sexual abuse may also be committed by a person under the age of 18 when that person is either significantly older than the victim or when the perpetrator is in a position of power and control over the victim.' This definition covers any participation in sexual activity by a dependent, developmentally immature child who is unable to comprehend the nature of the activity and give consent. It includes pornographic photography and filming of children for titillation.

3. Emotional abuse

This is very difficult to define. In a general sense it could be said that emotional abuse is a failure to provide an emotionally satisfying environment in which the child can thrive and develop. Children who are ignored, rejected or terrorised could be said to be emotionally abused. Involving a child in occult practices may be construed as a form of emotional abuse. Emotional abuse can cause failure to thrive, short stature, developmental delay and educational difficulty. There are cross-cultural differences in child rearing. It is incumbent that these be considered before unusual practices be designated as emotional abuse.

4. Neglect

This can be defined as a failure to provide the necessities of life for the child. These include food, clothing, warmth, stimulation, medical treatment, care and supervision. Exposure of the child to danger is an aspect of neglect.

Incidence

The terms incidence and prevalence are often confused. Incidence means the number of new cases over a given period, usually a year. Prevalence means the number of cases in the population at a given moment in time. The increasing media attention given to child abuse conveys the impression that both the incidence and prevalence of child abuse are increasing. There is no firm evidence that this apparent increase is real. Figures on the incidence of child abuse generally occasion much controversy. This is to be expected bearing in mind that most child abuse takes place behind closed doors and that definitions vary. The incidence of child abuse (excluding sexual abuse) in the United Kingdom is generally reckoned to be about 1 in 1000 of which there is a 10% mortality. The NSPCC estimates about 150–200 deaths due to child maltreatment and neglect each year in England and Wales, many being unrecognised as due to child abuse. Shown in Figure 1.1 are the annual child protection registrations and deregistrations in England since 1989 together with the composite number on the register. In the most recent year (1992) 38 600 children were registered. This represents a 15% reduction on the previous year and may be related to regulations and working practices connected with the Children Act (1989) which was implemented in October 1991. It should be emphasised that child abuse registers represent only the reported incidence and not the actual incidence which is unknown. Shown in Table 1.1 are the categories by which children were registered. Some were registered under more than one category. About a quarter of children on child protection registers are looked after by the Local Authority or are under a Supervision Order.

In the USA the Department of Health and Human Services figures

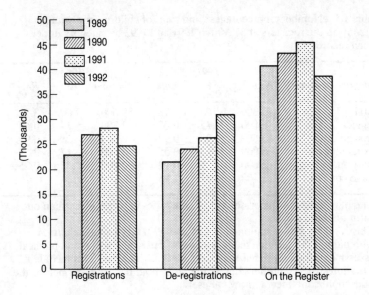

Figure 1.1 Registrations to and deregistrations from the child protection registers during the years ended 31 March 1989–1992, and the numbers on the register at 31 March each year. (*Source*: Department of Health, London.)

(1988) for the estimated number of recognised cases is 5.7 per 1000 children under 18. Between 1000 and 2000 children die each year from child abuse. The incidence in the USA has recently been rising. In a survey of maltreatment of children born to teenage mothers in the 1960s and 1980s, Leventhal found a similar incidence. This suggests that national figures of increased incidence reflect increased reporting rather than actual incidence. There is no accurate estimate of the incidence of sexual abuse in the United Kingdom. The definition is wide ranging from inappropriate fondling to frank intercourse. The diversity of activity renders the establishment of a true prevalence virtually impossible. Frequent reports in the media are probably the tip of an iceberg. Many adults admit to having been sexually abused as children, others are too scarred by the experience to talk about it. The coercive and secretive nature of child sexual abuse mitigates against disclosure by the dependent vulnerable child.

Child abuse and social class

Kempe's Department in Denver were the first to propagate the idea that child abuse occurred in all social groups and that it was distributed proportionately among the total population. The vast majority of children on child abuse registers are in the lowest social classes.

Table 1.1 Numbers, percentages* and rates of children and young persons on the registers at 31 March 1991 and 1992 by category under which recorded.

Category of abuse	1991 Number	1991 %	1991 Rate	1992 Number	1992 %	1992 Rate
Total	45 300	100	4.18	38 600	100	3.52
Neglect	6 800	15	0.63	7 300	19	0.67
Physical injury	10 600	23	0.97	10 900	28	0.99
Sexual abuse	6 000	13	0.55	6 500	17	0.59
Emotional abuse	2 600	6	0.24	2 800	7	0.25
Grave concern†	21 100	47	1.94	13 100	34	1.20

* The percentage incorporates mixed categories in which more than one form of abuse exists.

† This category was abandoned in October 1991. It included children who did not fall into the main categories, but where social and medical assessments indicated that they were at significant risk. This included situations where another child in the household had been harmed or the household contained a known abuser.

Numbers, percentages and rates per 1000 population aged under 18
Source: Department of Health, London.

This paradox is explained by the fact that there is little detection and reporting of child abuse in other classes. As recently as 1992 Creighton wrote: 'The children of the middle classes are less likely to come to the attention of these agencies than the poor and disadvantaged. There is also some evidence that levels of suspicion in professionals are affected by socio economic status.'

The work of David Finkelhor in the USA among the victims of child sexual abuse would support this view. He was unable to find any class or racial difference. Pelton regards the classlessness of child abuse as a myth. He argues that child abuse and neglect is strongly related to poverty both in terms of prevalence and severity. However, this is not to say that the problem does not occur in other classes. It would be my view that insofar as physical abuse and neglect are concerned Pelton is correct.

Features of perpetrators of child abuse

Most children are abused by a parent or cohabitee. Those incidents not involving a parent or cohabitee are generally committed by a custodian such as a foster parent, babysitter, relative or friend. These individuals are drawn from all sections of society, but the vast majority are from the poorest section, where deprivation and stress are most prevalent. They have poor coping mechanisms and are especially vulnerable to stress. They often have a disorganised, chaotic lifestyle with frequent changes of address and partners. Failed clinic appointments for their children and poor immunisation records owe much to their way of life.

Immaturity, impulsivity and poor frustration tolerance are common traits. Attitudes to behaviour are rigid and inflexible. Expectations of the child are unrealistically high. A number of abusers have had a punitive upbringing themselves and mistakenly believe that the treatment meted out to the child is 'normal discipline'. Because attitudes to behaviour and discipline are nurtured in childhood it is not uncommon for abuse to be passed from one generation to another.

Abusers may be educationally delayed and often have little concept of child development and the basic requirements of normal child care. Expectations may be inconsistent with developmental age. A high percentage have personality disorders. They have a low self-esteem and are unable to develop warm, trusting relationships. As a consequence they become socially isolated, often lacking support of friends or family. Depression may hinder a close emotional attachment to the child. There may be a history of alcohol or drug addiction, or crime, particularly deceit and violence. Many are unmarried and if married there is frequent marital disharmony with accompanying violence.

Common stresses

These are frequently found in the poorest part of society and include poor housing, overcrowding, unemployment and financial hardship. Other stresses may be illness, bereavement, divorce or separation. In this social incubus a trivial event may precipitate the abusive episode. Such events include disconnection of electricity or gas due to failure to pay bills, a parental argument or fight, or excessive crying by the child, particularly when intercourse is interrupted.

Attempts to predict or prevent child abuse have borne little fruit owing to the complex inter-relationship between environment, abuser and victim.

Features of victims of child abuse

Most children who are abused have no distinguishing features, but are often perceived by the abuser as different. It is common for one child in a family, or even one of twins, to be abused. The reasons for this subconscious perception are complex. They may include an unplanned pregnancy causing a change in relationships, a financial burden, interrupted employment or educational prospects. Most abused children are less than three, some of whom are stubborn, very demanding and 'hyperactive'. Abuse is more common in children with a mental or physical handicap or a chronic illness, supporting the perception of their being different. The prevalence is higher in children who have been separated from mothers in early life due to prematurity or maternal illness. This reason is not purely a failure of 'bonding' as was once thought. Happy, stable relationships frequently occur when parents have never seen their children in early childhood. Victims of abuse frequently find themselves in a situation where they are cared for by a non-biological parent.

Physical violence on teenagers generally arises out of friction over matters such as discipline. In a fit of pique loss of self-control by an irate adult results in physical injuries which in their extent and situation are abusive. Parents are unable to cope with the natural rebellion of the teens, friction often being enhanced when the child is more intelligent than the parents or is a stepchild.

Sexual abuse

Most perpetrators of sexual abuse are members of the family or known to the child. These may be a friend, babysitter, cousin, parent or grandparent. Females may be perpetrators but the vast majority are males, some having been sexually abused themselves. Sexual activity with children sometimes starts in the abuser's teens. With the exception of a few sadists and psychopaths most are normal individuals. Their paraphilia (sexual perversion), which is well disguised, is the only feature which distinguishes them from other members of society. The psychodynamics of the sexual arousal of adults by children is as yet an unresolved psychiatric issue. The abuser is aware of his wrongdoing but comes to terms with it by a system of distorted rationalisation. For example, he may believe that the child actually wants to have sex because she does not resist. His activities may be rationalised as providing the child with sex education. Not surprisingly men with these tendencies often drift into activities or occupations involving close contact with children. Coercion is usually achieved by threats rather than physical means. Children are told to 'keep the secret or else'. Many men are able to control their sexual interest in children until they are overtaken by events. Such precipitating events are marital problems, maternal depression and absence of the wife from the home due to illness or her employment. Alcohol and drugs are sometimes a factor in lowering inhibitions. A frequent feature in these homes is the poor relationship between mother and daughter, the mother being unable to protect the daughter. Sexual abuse is more common in homes where the daughter is cared for by a stepmother. Many mothers were sexually abused as children and have a punitive attitude to sexual matters; children are seldom provided with any sex education. The mothers are generally less well educated and less assertive than the men. Many are aware of the relationship but ignore it as a way of preventing the break up of the family. Others, because of implicit trust and skilled deception by the man do not realise what is happening and are truly dumbfounded when abuse comes to light. Some mothers respond immediately by believing and supporting the child. Others find it hard to believe and accuse the child of lying or fantasising. In the face of denial by the perpetrator the child feels helpless, guilty and dejected. A retraction is made which is quickly accepted leaving the child vulnerable to further abuse and long-term psychological harm.

In summary, David Finkelhor has listed four preconditions that need to be met before sexual abuse can occur. They are:

1. A potential perpetrator needs to have the motivation to sexually abuse a child.
2. He must have the ability to overcome his own internal inhibitions and moral standards by acting on that motivation.
3. External impediments to the commission of the act need to be overcome. A protective parent would be such an impediment.
4. The resistance of the child needs to be overcome by seduction or coercion.

Sex rings

A sex ring is said to exist when children are sexually abused by one or more adults. There are three types of ring, a common feature to each is the use of pornography (child and adult) as a technique to normalise adult–child sex, or for the purpose of demonstrating the type of pose or sexual activity expected of the child.

(a) *The solo ring*. In this type of ring the adult knows the children or has a position of authority over them. Contact with the children is made through the adult's occupation, a leisure activity or because he lives near them. One child may introduce him to the other children. Children are generally recruited by bribery and usually know one another and each is aware of the sexual activity of the other. Children involved in solo sex rings are mainly of similar age, preschool, prepubescent, adolescent. The latter may be introduced to prostitution by the adult.

(b) *'Friendly' paedophile ring*. Paedophiles communicate with each other by exchanging pictures of children and/or child contacts. There is a feeling of comraderie between these individuals and the exchange is undertaken in a spirit of friendship, hence the name.

(c) *'Commercial' paedophile ring*. Unlike the 'friendly' paedophile ring the 'commercial' ring is a highly organised business network in which adults recruit children for the provision of sexual services and pornography for customers. Communication within the network is covert so as not to fall foul of the law.

Sex rings have a damaging psychological impact on children, particularly when participation is prolonged. The longer the child is in the ring the more the socially deviant behaviour becomes perceived as the norm. The psychodynamics of the ring are such that each child by being aware of the activities of the other becomes locked in. By being 'incriminated' there is strong pressure not to betray. Moreover, there is a positive side in that the child is being rewarded. Rewards are commonly such things as sweets, money, drugs or alcohol. To the insecure child the attention received by posing for pictures may be very appealing. The adult maintains the coherence of the ring by acting as the benevolent one and often uses group members against one another as part of a 'divide and rule' strategy.

Ritual abuse

There have been a few reports in the media of sexual abuse of children taking place among satanic cults. Information about ritualistic abuse is not well documented. The publicity given to this form of abuse by the media probably far exceeds its true prevalence. It can be defined as follows: 'Ritual abuse is one or more types of abuse, physical, sexual and emotional, combined with a systematic use of symbols, ceremonies and machinations designed and orchestrated to attain a malevolent effect.'

See Acknowledgements page for updated information.

Institutional abuse

When institutions fail to meet the physical and emotional needs of children this can be defined as institutional abuse. Examples are:

1. Inappropriate removal of children from families.
2. Unacceptable 'methods' of removal. Surprise visits in the dead of night or dawn raids are to be condemned.
3. Repeated intrusive interviews and examinations.
4. Inappropriate negative labelling of families.
5. Abuse of children in residential institutions. There have recently been a number of Inquiries into the abuse of children in Local Authority residential homes. The clear message emanating from those Inquiries is that the potential for abuse is directly related to the extent of regular, rigorous and effective monitoring.

Legal abuse

The process of law as it affects children has in the past been disjointed, lengthy and cumbersome. Caught up in this farrago has been the child, the 'object of professional concern'. In the 1980s there was much debate about the harmful effect on the child caused by delays in the resolution of legal matters. As a consequence one of the overriding principles of the Children Act 1989 is the speeding up of the legal process.

Medical abuse

There are many children in hospitals who have unnecessary, often painful, invasive medical procedures. Painful procedures are often performed on children without the provision of pain relief. There is a common misbelief that babies do not feel pain or if they do 'it is soon forgotten'. Because children are unlikely to resist there is potential for them to be exploited in medical research. In the past many unethical studies have been undertaken on children.

Circumcision, male and female, falls under the rubric of medical abuse. Female circumcision is illegal in Britain, while male circumcision is only performed on the NHS when it is medically indicated. In the USA three-quarters of male infants are circumcised despite the view of the American Academy of Pediatrics that there is no valid medical reason for routine circumcision. Almost all such circumcisions are undertaken without analgesia or anaesthesia. Some would regard male circumcision as the commonest form of child abuse in America.

Societal abuse

This is a matter for governments and politicians. It is, however, the duty of child care professionals to act as advocates for children and to campaign on their behalf. There are parts of the world where children provide 'slave labour' in appalling and often dangerous conditions. In some places children are under arms, in others they are detained and tortured. That these practices are not always condemned is a matter of political expediency and frequently a lack of will. One can only be bemused by reports of beef or butter 'mountains' in the EEC when there are daily reports of children dying of hunger in Africa.

Further reading

1. Kempe CH, Silverman FN, Steele BF, Droegemueller W, Silver HK. The Battered Child Syndrome. *Journal of the American Medical Association* 1962; **181**: 17–24.

2. Pelton LH. Child abuse and neglect: the myth of classlessness. *American Journal of Orthopsychiatry* 1978; **48**: 608–17.
3. Finkelhor D. *Sexually Abused Children*. New York: Free Press, 1979.
4. Summit RC. Child abuse accommodation syndrome. *Child Abuse and Neglect* 1983; **7**: 177.
5. Finkelhor D. *Child Abuse – New Theory and Research*. New York: Free Press, 1984.
6. AMA diagnostic and treatment guidelines concerning child abuse and neglect. *JAMA* 1985; **254**: 796.
7. Parton N. *The Politics of Child Abuse*. London, Macmillan, 1985.
8. Lynch MA. Child abuse before Kempe: an historical literature review. *Child Abuse and Neglect* 1985; **9**: 7–15.
9. Helfer RE, Kempe RS. *The Battered Child*. Chicago: University of Chicago Press, 1987.
10. Anonymous. Dilemmas of child sexual abuse. *Paediatric and Perinatal Epidemiology* 1988; **2**: 107.
11. Butler-Sloss E. *Report of the Enquiry into Child Abuse in Cleveland 1987*. London: Her Majesty's Stationery Office, 1988.
12 Barker P. *Basic Child Psychiatry* (Chapter 18, Child abuse and neglect). London: Blackwell, 1988.
13. Fuller AK. Child molestation and pedophilia – an overview for the physician. *JAMA* 1989; **461**: 602.
14. Reece RM. Child abuse. *Pediatric Clinics of North America* 1990, volume 37, number 4.
15. Masako T, Matsui I, Kobayashi N. Child abuse of one pair of twins in Japan. *Lancet* 1990; **336**: 1298.
16. De Jong AR, Finkel MA. Sexual abuse of children. *Current Problems in Pediatrics* 1990, volume 20, number 9.
17 Anonymous. Cycles of violence in child physical abuse. *Lancet* 1991; **338**: 88.
18. Tate T. *Children for the Devil*. London: Methuen, 1991.
19. *Child Abuse. A Study of Inquiry Reports 1980–1989*. London: Her Majesty's Stationery Office, 1991.
20. Creighton SJ. *Trends in Child Abuse*. London: National Society for the Prevention of Cruelty to Children, 1992.
21. Ludwig S, Kornberg AE. *Child Abuse. A Medical Reference*. London: Churchill Livingstone, 1992.
22. Leventhal JM, Horwitz SM, Rude C, Stier DM. Maltreatment of children born to teenage mothers: a comparison between the 1960s and 1980s. *Journal of Pediatrics* 1993; **122**: 314–19.
23. McClain PW, Sacks JJ, Froehlke RG, Ewigman BG. Estimates of fatal child abuse and neglect, United States, 1979 through 1988. *Pediatrics* 1993; **91**: 338–43.
24. Westcott HL. *Abuse of Children and Adults with Disabilities*. London: National Society for the Prevention of Cruelty to Children, 1993.
25. Kelley SJ. Ritualistic Abuse of Children. In: Hobbs CJ, Wynne JM eds. *Child Abuse*. London: Baillière Tindall, 1993.

2 Prevention of child abuse

In discussing the prevention of child abuse it is appropriate first to consider the prevailing social and economic climate. In Britain we have recently experienced the worst recession since the war, three million people being unemployed. Thousands of families are homeless or live in substandard accommodation. Poverty is rife. More than one in four children are born out of wedlock and one in three marriages ends in divorce. Juvenile crime is endemic and drug abuse among the young is increasing.

Can child abuse be prevented? The prevention of child abuse is a forlorn hope. It is a complex, unpredictable problem deeply embedded in human nature. While it is most prevalent in the bottom stratum of society it would be facile to imagine that the pouring of money into the most underprivileged part of the community would prevent child abuse. In Britain, although vast resources are currently directed to the prevention of child abuse, there is still little scientific evidence pointing to the value of such efforts. The lack of proof should not necessarily denigrate those efforts which are both morally and politically correct.

The following observations are pertinent to the planning of a prevention programme:

1. There is no prediction formula which can accurately distinguish the abuser from the non-abuser.
2. Child abuse has many deep-rooted causes and the most successful prevention programme is likely to be multidimensional rather than one which addresses one or two specific issues.
3. Child abuse is heavily weighted at the lower end of the social spectrum. Primary prevention directed at the general population is likely to have high cost implications in that information will go to people who do not require it.
4. Intrusive family programmes are likely to be met with hostility. In Britain parenthood continues to be construed in terms of ownership; there is widespread parental belief that children are 'property' to be handled as parents choose.

Conventionally, prevention programmes are categorised as primary, secondary and tertiary.

Primary prevention

These strategies are directed at the total population in an effort to diminish the incidence of child abuse. They do not focus on risk factors or risk groups. Examples of primary prevention are midwifery, health visiting and general practitioner child health surveillance services in which all children are reviewed at set intervals.

In Britain primary prevention is well organised. All antenatal clinics provide parentcraft classes which are available for both mothers and fathers. After birth midwives visit homes for the first month, following which child care monitoring and home visiting are undertaken by health visitors. These programmes, together with general practitioner child health surveillance, afford a good opportunity for parental advice and for the child's health and development to be monitored.

Another example of primary prevention is the school-based strategy for the prevention of child sexual abuse. These 'Say No!' campaigns have led to an increase in disclosures but few other positive benefits.

Secondary prevention

Specific subsets of the population known to be at risk of child abuse are targeted. Typically these are directed at the poorest members of our society and those who have least family support such as single parents. An example of secondary prevention is the provision of Local Authority nurseries for children in most need. In some of these nurseries parents are encouraged to visit, are taught parenting skills and are instructed on child development. The training process is sometimes extended to the family environment by outreach workers visiting the homes.

The best evaluated secondary prevention strategy in connection with home visiting was that of Olds in the USA.[1,2] He identified high risk families and home visits were undertaken both in the prenatal and postnatal periods. The main components of the programme were: parent education concerning fetal and infant development; enhancement of informal supports available by encouraging friends and relatives to be involved in the home visits; and linkage of family members with health care and social services including day care and job training. Olds found that in the highest risk group (poor, teenaged, single mothers) there was a significant reduction in incidents of child abuse/neglect.

A secondary prevention study targeted at high risk families was undertaken by Lealman in Bradford, England.[3] The postnatal interventions were: contact with a social worker after discharge from the hospital; creation of a 'drop in' centre one day a week; provision of

Table 2.1 Prevention and intervention strategies.

Individual	Family	Community	Culture
1. Psychotherapeutic help for abusive parents	1. Marriage counselling	1. Provision of good housing and health and social services	1. Enact child protection legislation
2. Treatment for abused child	2. Help with managing home budgets	2. Train professionals to recognise abuse	2. Prohibit corporal punishment in schools
3. Alcohol and drug rehabilitation programmes	3. Parenting skills training	3. Provision of a child protection service (Local Authority/NSPCC)	3. Promote alternative forms of discipline; away from corporal punishment
4. Job search assistance	4. Home safety training	4. Screen child care personnel/foster and adoptive parents	4. Campaign to increase public awareness
5. Stress relief measures	5. Antenatal parentcraft training	5. Establish crisis telephone lines	5. Audit prevalence and undertake research into prevention
	6. Health visiting	6. Facilitate community support groups	
		7. Provision of foster/respite care for families in need	
		8. Provision of family planning and immunisation clinics	

the project secretary's telephone number. Lealman found that these supportive measures did not prevent abuse. Those who needed and received the most attention from social workers and health visitors fared worse. The difference in outcome between the American and British studies is probably reflected in the multidimensional nature of the intervention in the former.

Tertiary prevention

This is an after-the-fact strategy which is intended to prevent a recurrence or to minimise the psychological damage. Besides therapy such measures include identifying and reporting child abuse, following abuse procedures and resorting to the courts if necessary.

Belsky proposed a conceptual model for integrating the diverse theories on the cause of child abuse.[4] The Belsky paradigm is a 'social psychological phenomenon' with multiple forces at work at four levels: the individual, family, community and culture. Rosenberg has highlighted the importance of this model in the prevention of child abuse.[5] A comprehensive prevention programme based on it is shown in Table 2.1.

The best prevention programmes incorporate interventions at various levels in the environment. The only hope of abuse prevention lies in a long-term commitment to such programmes.

> Development is a continuous process; experiences at any given age are affected by and built on experiences that have come before. Intervention at later stages of life can no more wipe out a history of disadvantage than can a brief early intervention inoculate a child against continuing disadvantage. The most successful intervention should comprise a series of dovetailed programs, independently available as the need requires, with each appropriate for a particular stage of development – prenatal, infancy and toddlerhood, preschool and early elementary school years, middle childhood, and adolescence.
>
> Zigler and Berman 1983[6]

References

1. Olds DL, Henderson CR, Tatelbaum R, Chamberlin R. Prenatal care and outcomes of pregnancy: a randomized trial of nurse home visitation. *Pediatrics* 1986: **77**; 16–28.
2. Olds DL, Henderson CR, Chamberlin R, Tatelbaum R. Preventing child abuse and neglect: a randomised trial of nurse home visitation. *Pediatrics* 1986: **78**; 65–78.
3. Lealman GT, Phillips JM, Haigh D, Stone J, Ord-Smith C. Prediction and prevention of child abuse – an empty hope? *Lancet* 1983: **1**; 1423–4.
4. Belsky J. Child maltreatment: an ecological integration. *American Psychologist* 1980: **35**; 320–35.
5. Rosenberg MS, Repucci ND. Primary prevention of child abuse. *Journal*

of Consulting and Clinical Psychology 1985: **53**; 576–85.
6. Zigler E, Berman W. Discerning the future of early childhood intervention. *American Psychologist* 1983: **38**; 894–906.

Further reading

Dubowitz H. Prevention of child maltreatment: what is known. *Pediatrics* 1989: **83**; 570–7.

Dubowitz H. Pediatrician's role in preventing child maltreatment. *Pediatric Clinics of North America* 1990: **37**; 989–1002.

Olds DL, Henderson CR, Kitzman H. Does Prenatal and Infancy Nurse Home Visitation Have Enduring Effects on Qualities of Parental Caregiving and Child Health at 25–50 months of Life? *Pediatrics* 1994: 89–98.

Willis DJ, Holden EW, Rosenberg M. *Prevention of Child Maltreatment*. New York: John Wiley and Sons, 1992.

3 The history

Before the history is taken it is always worthwhile noting the source of referral. Such information may be helpful in that the attitude and reaction of parents might be anticipated. A parent who has instigated a visit to the Casualty Department is less likely to be belligerent than one brought to the hospital by a social worker or the police. The date, time and names and relationships of those present during the interview should be recorded. The sequence of events should then be noted in a stepwise fashion legibly in the casenotes. The more detail the better, as this information may be required at a case conference or a court case months later. The time, site and circumstances surrounding the injury should be documented. Those present at the time of the injury and their relationship to the child should be recorded. Attention should be given to the timing and sequence of events that followed the injury.

The history should be taken in a quiet room where parents can be guaranteed privacy. The middle of a busy Casualty Department is not the place to conduct the interview. Ideally if the child is over three and able to articulate, he should be interviewed separately. Many children feel apprehensive, guilty and are bewildered at what is happening. Their apprehension is understandable as even in the most abusive homes children do feel a sense of security. Information from these children can often best be obtained by the use of non-leading questions.

It is usually very difficult to interview parents separately without appearing too inquisitory and arousing hostility. The history should be taken as soon as possible after the incident before there is chance of collusion and a change of story. If both parents are present the interviewer should try to assess how they relate to each other and the child. The doctor should start the interview by explaining that he is there to help. His attitude should be caring and not pejorative. Parental reactions vary considerably. Some are submissive, polite and co-operative, while others are belligerent, abusive and resistant. Scapegoats readily come to mind. The concern of the parents for the injury often helps in deciding whether the injury is accidental or abuse. Overconcern for a minor injury or underconcern for a more serious injury would be suggestive of abuse. There may be failure to acknowledge the seriousness of the injury or refusal of hospital admission.There may be few questions about treatment or prognosis. Some leave the hospital before a history can be taken.

In addition to a full social history other details will be required depending on the child's age. A feeding history is particularly important in the case of failure to thrive or neglect. A developmental history may provide evidence of emotional abuse. Insight into sources of friction in the family may be obtained by asking about perceived behaviour problems of the child and difficulties with bowel and bladder control. Information about immunisation status should be sought – neglected children may not have been immunised. Previous visits to the Accident and Emergency Department and the reasons should be noted. Abused children frequently have a history of a number of attendances with accidents or ingestions. Inquiry should be made about the medical (including psychiatric) history of the parents and any medication they might be taking. Epilepsy in a parent may result in a child sustaining an unexplained injury.

The hallmarks of a child abuse history are:

1. *Unexplained injury*. It is common for parents who have abused a child to provide no explanation. At times a vague explanation lacking commitment or the detail one could reasonably expect is proffered. Such explanations are frequently punctuated with 'may have', 'might have' or 'could have'. After a genuine accident parents can invariably provide precise details. The inability to provide an explanation is incriminating and strongly suggests abuse.
2. *Discrepant history*. The history may be discrepant in that the child or one or other parent gives a different version of events. There may also be a discrepancy between the type or severity of the injuries and the facts. Such an example is a child with multiple bruises of differing ages who is said to have slipped and fallen in the snow. The histories provided are often implausible and sometimes bizarre. For example parents may explain bite marks on a child's arm as the result of having been caught in the vacuum cleaner.
3. *Delay in seeking medical help*. This is a common feature of parental reaction after child abuse, but is not always the case. The reason for delay will be unexplained, false or a feeble excuse will be given. For example a child with a serious burn may not have been brought to the hospital 'because he stopped crying'. When there is suspicion of delay cognisance should be given to the maturity and intellectual capacity of the carer. A young, intellectually dull mother may perceive the severity of an injury differently from her older, brighter counterpart.

The credence given to the history is of the utmost importance in deciding if an injury is a genuine accident. It may occasionally be necessary for the physician to visit the scene in order to assure himself of the veracity of the history. Genuine accidents do sometimes occur in unusual and unexpected ways. No doctor is omniscient and errors of judgement can be made. One should not be reticent about seeking the views of colleagues.

Child sexual abuse

The interview is usually undertaken jointly by a police officer (usually a woman) and a social worker and should be video recorded. The interviewer may be required to give evidence in court. A police officer is necessary for the collection of forensic evidence but may be accompanied by another professional such as a psychologist, psychiatrist or paediatrician. As most children who are sexually abused do not have physical evidence the history will form the basis of the case against the perpetrator. It is a prerequisite of those interviewing the child that they be skilled in interviewing techniques and that they have a good knowledge of the normal developmental patterns of children. The interviewer should have an understanding of the way children are sexually abused and the impact of such abuse. Punctillious attention to detail is required. Interviewing a child with sensitivity, empathy and equanimity is a skill which is learned. Such interviewing is best undertaken by those with special training. It is essential that professionals undertaking such interviews be well versed in the information set out in the Home Office document *Memorandum of Good Practice*.

The interview should be held at a venue where the child feels safe and comfortable. In addition to recording facilities there should be drawing utensils, anatomically correct dolls and toys. Too many toys, however, may be a distraction from the task in hand. The interview usually lasts one to two hours and should not be interrupted. Before commencement the child should be given food and a drink and taken to the toilet. She should then be shown where her parents will be waiting at the end of the interview. It is now generally agreed that children should be interviewed alone. The presence of a parent is likely to pass on subtle cues to the child thereby contaminating the evidence. The exception to this rule is when a child has disclosed to a teacher or some other ally, then the supportive ally may accompany the child.

Sgroi has said that the purpose of the interview is to address the following:

1. Did the alleged perpetrator have access to the child? Was there opportunity for discreet interaction?
2. How were the activities presented to the child?

3. To what extent did the activities progress and what was their frequency over time? Most sexual abuse of children is not a 'one off'. The water is first tested by the perpetrator and gradually activities progress and develop.
4. What techniques has the perpetrator employed in order to secure the participation of the child and the maintenance of secrecy? These may be threats, bribery or coercion.
5. What feelings did the child have while experiencing the abuse?
6. What were the circumstances which brought about the disclosure? Was the disclosure made by accident or design?
7. What are the feelings and expectations of the child now that the disclosure has been made?

The extent to which these questions can be answered depends on the child's age, developmental level and ability to articulate. The interview is best conducted with non leading questions, but these may be necessary when the child blocks. Evidence obtained by direct questioning is likely to be viewed with suspicion by the courts. An excerpt from *Memorandum of Good Practice* states:

> Leading questions would not normally be allowed if the child was giving his or her evidence in chief live during criminal proceedings and it is to be expected that such questioning in a video recorded interview would be excluded by the court. The greatest care must therefore be taken when questioning the child about central matters which are likely to be in dispute.

The interview should proceed at the child's pace avoiding pressure. A rapport may first need to be achieved before the child will disclose; this may not occur until a second or subsequent interview.

The interview should start with an introduction. The child should be told that the interviewer frequently talks to children like her, children with worries because things have happened to them. It may be necessary to tell the child that many children are afraid to talk about things that have happened to them and if that is the case the interviewer will understand. The child is then allowed a period of free play lasting 5–10 minutes. The ice can then be broken by getting the child to do line drawings of the family or by undressing the dolls. This enables the interviewer to establish the child's names for the genitalia and these names can then be used by the interviewer. A discussion about 'private' and 'public' parts should follow to assess the child's perception of such things. The interviewer may wish to distinguish the difference between these parts by alluding to those being covered by a swimming costume as 'private'.

The next phase of the interview is the exploration of the child's concepts of good and bad touching. Touching which is ordinary and appropriate (e.g. a cuddle) being described as 'nice'. 'Bad' is defined as not nice or inappropriate. 'Ichy' might be used to describe touches which the child finds funny or confusing and do not fit into the nice or bad category. It is at this point in the interview that handling the dolls by the child can be gradually introduced as a way of demonstrating nice and bad touches. Many children are fearful of the dolls and need to be coaxed.

The dolls are then named e.g. 'Mummy' doll, 'Daddy' doll, 'Uncle Joe' (alleged perpetrator), etc. The child should then be asked if she has any touches from Uncle Joe and she should be asked to demonstrate them. The interviewer should then ask 'What sort of touching is that?' Time should then be allowed for a response and the child's reactions carefully observed. If no response is forthcoming probing may be needed. Having got a disclosure further questioning should try to elicit the scene, time and the whereabouts of other members of the household. Details of the room, the bed and clothing the child or perpetrator wore should be sought. It may be necessary to ask questions such as 'Was it dark?', 'Before or after your bath?', 'Did it start before your sister was born?' Precise information about the nature of the acts performed and the number of individuals (perpetrators) should be obtained. Children should be asked to express the sensations and feelings they experienced during the specific alleged activities. Details such as the taste of semen being salty would greatly enhance the validity of the testimony.

Once the child has demonstrated with drawings or dolls what has or has not happened the interviewer should briefly cover the same ground again as a way of recapping. It should also be regarded as a test of consistency.

The child can then be helped to dress the dolls and in 'winding down' the interview it is very important to stress the following:

1. It is never the child's fault. The adult behaved wrongly in doing this to her.
2. The interviewer should emphasise that the child is believed implicitly. There is no reason whatever to doubt the veracity of a young child in allegations of this nature. The situation with regard to older children and teenagers may be different.
3. If there has been abuse the child should be told that the perpetrator will be given some help so that he desists from such things. If no abuse has been shown the child should be praised for being helpful, and for clarifying matters.

The interview format presented here is just one way of dealing with the problem. There is room for flexibility and there will be variations of the theme from one interviewer to another depending on the child and the circumstances. Older children may wish to draw, but dolls can sometimes be useful when these children wish to demonstrate what has happened rather than verbalise. It should be pointed out that the use of dolls in an interview of this nature is a subject which occasions much controversy. From the legal perspective courts both in Britain and the USA would not regard the interpretation of the child's behaviour with the dolls as a reliable method of proving or disproving abuse. An excerpt from *Memorandum of Good Practice* states: 'In the main, genitalled dolls should only be used as an adjunct to the interview to establish the meaning of terms used by the child once the child has finished his or her free narrative account, and the general substance of his or her evidence is reasonably clear.'

There is no necessity to obtain written or oral consent for a video recorded interview, however it is strongly recommended that oral consent be obtained from the child (if of sufficient understanding) or a parent or carer where possible. An explanation of the advantages in making such a recording should accompany any request for consent. At the start of the interview the use of the video camera should be pointed out to the child.

Further reading

1. Ellerstein NS. *Child Abuse and Neglect – A Medical Reference*. New York: John Wiley and Sons, 1981.
2. Sgroi S. *Handbook of Clinical Intervention in Child Sexual Abuse*. Lexington, Mass: Lexington Books, 1982.
3. Kempe RS and Kempe CH. *The Common Secret – Sexual Abuse of Children and Adolescents*. New York: W H Freeman & Co, 1984.
4. Helfer RS, Kempe RE. *The Battered Child*. Chicago: University of Chicago Press, 1987.
5. Bentovim A. *Child Sexual Abuse within the Family, Assessment and Treatment*. London: Butterworth & Co, 1988.
6. Goldberg CG, Yates A. The use of anatomically correct dolls in the evaluation of sexually abused children. *American Journal of Disease of Children* 1990; **144**: 1334–6.
7. Seidl T. Special interviewing techniques. In: Ludwig S, Kornberg AE eds. *Child Abuse. A Medical Reference*. London: Churchill Livingstone, 1992.
8. Jones DPH. *Interviewing the Sexually Abused Child*. London: Royal College of Psychiatrists. Gaskell, 1992.
9. *Memorandum of Good Practice*, London: Her Majesty's Stationery Office, 1992.

4 The examination

Before the examination the doctor will usually have details of the mode of referral and history. Consent to medical examination and photography should be obtained from the parents or, in some cases where the child is of sufficient understanding, the child. In the case of sexual abuse consent should be obtained in writing. Because it may not be in the parental interest for the child to be examined the doctor should emphasise that he acts independently and does not represent the police or Social Services. He should also tell them that he will provide a verbal report when the examination is complete and that the report will not differ from any written report that may be required. Parents who are unco-operative and resistant will usually relent when informed that under the Children Act 1989 an order can be obtained for the examination of the child. This should not be put across as a threat but it should be pointed out that it would be in their interest to concede. The need for photography should be portrayed as being in both their interest and that of the child. They should be told that photographs circumvent the need for further examinations and that copies of the photographs would be available to them or their legal adviser should they wish to obtain an independent medical opinion.

The examination should be undertaken in a room with good lighting and toys where the child would feel safe and comfortable. In cases of child sexual abuse it is imperative that the examination of the child and the alleged perpetrator be undertaken in separate locations. Forensic evidence, based on Locard's principle that every contact leaves a trace, may depend on clothing fibres to establish contact between child and perpetrator. Such evidence could be vitiated by examination in the same place when cross-contamination of clothing fibres might occur. Extreme sensitivity is required as children are often frightened and those that have been sexually abused have feelings of being soiled or of 'damage' to their bodies. The child should be told that the doctor is going to 'check him over from top to toe' and will draw pictures of his marks. When it is over the 'cameraman' will take some pictures. Children who have been sexually abused will require a variation of this theme in age-appropriate language which will have been established during the taking of the history. The child should be accompanied by a parent, relative or supportive ally (e.g. a teacher). Older children should be given a choice about having a companion.

Children should be weighed and measured and the measurements recorded on centile charts. The date, time and names of those present during the examination should be recorded on 'body charts' (see Figures 4.1a and b) together with the injuries. Details of injuries such as colour, measurements, configuration, tenderness and broken skin

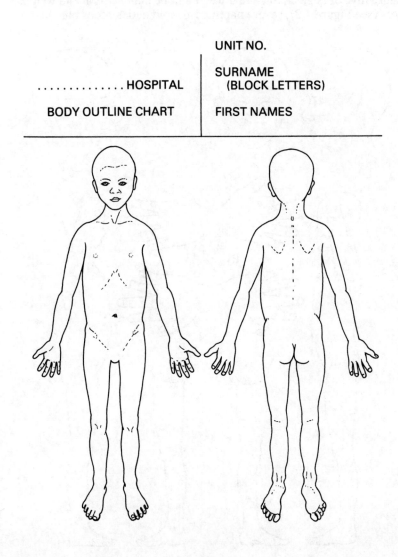

UNIT NO.

. . . . HOSPITAL

BODY OUTLINE CHART

SURNAME
(BLOCK LETTERS)

FIRST NAMES

Figure 4.1 (a) Body outline chart which is used for recording injuries.

should be recorded. Features very suggestive of abuse are injuries of different ages and types, for example burns and bruises. Attention to detail is very important. Cases frequently come to court many months after an incident when information committed to memory may have been lost.

The cleanliness of the child should be noted together with evidence suggestive of neglect. Such features might be malnutrition and weight loss (see Figure 4.2), severe nappy rash, cold oedematous blue hands

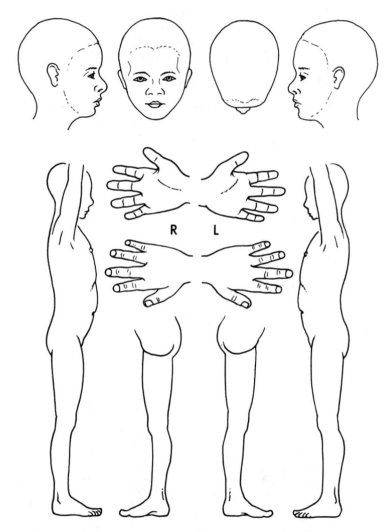

Figure 4.1 (b)   Body outline chart which is used for recording information.

and feet and elastic marks from clothing which is too tight. The demeanour of the child should be noted. Chronically abused children often have a dull, vacant stare known as 'frozen watchfulness' (see Figure 4.3). Others may exhibit gaze avoidance (see Figure 4.4). These children are frequently submissive, docile and do not cry easily. The nonchalant, submissive attitude of some girls who have been chronically sexually abused is readily apparent.

A child with an injury should have a full medical examination. An injury which is not readily apparent may come to light when it is noticed that the child is limping or not moving his limbs. Many of the children who are abused come from the deprived part of society and may need attention to their medical needs. Such needs might

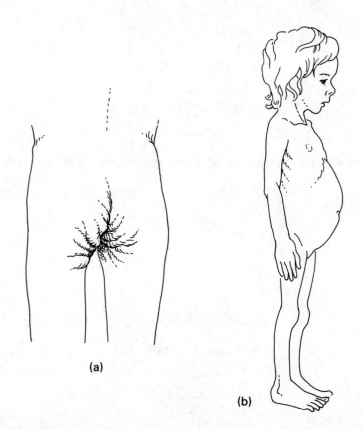

(a)

(b)

Figure 4.2 (a) Wasted buttocks and (b) 'pot belly' typical of malnutrition and neglect.

include the detection and treatment of lice, scabies, squint, dental caries and undescended testes.

Children who have been sexually abused frequently have other injuries and these children should always have a general examination in addition to an examination of the genitalia. There is controversy as to whether all children (mainly girls) should have a genital examination when there is evidence of abuse elsewhere. The prevailing view in Britain would seem to be that this should not be undertaken unless

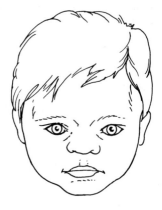

Figure 4.3 The typical stare of 'frozen watchfulness' of the chronically abused child.

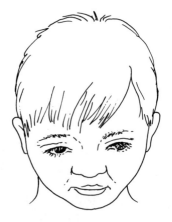

Figure 4.4 Gaze avoidance, a characteristic of some chronically abused children.

there are reasons for suspecting sexual abuse.

Prior to the examination, arrangements for the medical photographer to be available should be made. Where possible the photographer should be introduced to the child before the examination and should remain out of the room until he is required at the end. Having the photographer present avoids the child dressing and then undressing again. It also affords the physician the opportunity of showing the photographer the evidence worthy of photographing. While some doctors take their own photographs the standard required by the courts is such that this work is best undertaken by a professional. Photographs should show the name of the child and date. Rulers may be incorporated in the photographs so that a true impression of size can be obtained. With the possible exception of sexually abused children the face should be included in the photographs as a further means of identifying the child in the case of legal proceedings. Close-up colour photographs should be accompanied by distant photographs showing the size and situation of the injury in relation to other parts of the body. It is common for bruising to develop so that it is most intense a day or two after the injury. On such occasions it may be necessary for the child to be photographed again. Similarly, where there is contention about the timing of a burn a repeat photograph showing the stage of healing may be required.

Further reading

1. Glover S, Nicoll A, Pullan C. Deprivation hands and feet. *Archives of Disease in Childhood* 1985; **60**: 976.
2. Ricci LR. Photographing the physically abused child. Principles and practice. *American Journal of Diseases of Children* 1991; **145**: 275.
3. Flaherty EG, Weiss H. Medical evaluation of abused and neglected children. *American Journal of Diseases in Childhood* 1990; **144**: 330.
4. Ludwig S, Kornberg AE. *Child Abuse. A Medical Reference*. London: Churchill Livingstone, 1992.

5   Neglect and failure to gain weight (thrive)

What is neglect? The Collins English Dictionary defines it as 'to fail to give due care, attention or time to'. When the physical and/or emotional well-being of the child is placed in jeopardy as a result of parental action or lack thereof a state of neglect could be said to exist. The manifestations of neglect usually involve many aspects of child rearing. It is the duty of a responsible carer to provide for the basic needs of a young child. These needs can be categorised under the following headings:

1. Nutrition

Children who are neglected frequently receive inadequate calories (normal requirement 100–120 cal/kg/day in infancy) and fail to gain weight. Rarely, the opposite may occur. The parent unable correctly to perceive and satisfy the needs of the child uses food. The child is fed excessively creating an excess weight gain.

2. Health and hygiene

Neglected children are often not immunised. Parents do not respond to their health needs. When unwell, no medical attention is sought. Medical appointments are not kept and when accidents occur no action is taken. Caries is common as parents pay little attention to diet and dental hygiene. Visits to a dentist are seldom made. Children with squints may develop a lazy eye (amblyopia) as spectacles are not worn and eye patching instructions not carried out. The health of the child is not a big issue, many of the mothers having smoked or taken drugs or alcohol during pregnancy.

Neglected children are commonly dirty owing to infrequent baths. Lice, scabies and skin infections such as impetigo are often found. Many infants have severe napkin dermatitis from infrequent nappy changes.

3. Love and attention

Neglected children are seldom afforded the love and attention of a caring relationship. Typically when these children are admitted to hospital parents may not visit or make inquiries about the child, and many parents leave the hospital immediately, before the admitting doctor has the opportunity to take a history. When parents do visit they often seem to be more interested in socialising and ward activities than caring for the child. The lack of attention and stimulation frequently causes developmental delay. Children often have difficulty in socialising and speech is impaired. Self-stimulatory behaviours such as head banging, rocking and rumination are common. The vomiting caused by the latter is often attributed by the unwary to gastro-oesophageal reflux. The reaction of the child varies from the withdrawn 'frozen watchfulness' (Figure 4.3) to the child craving attention who reaches out to any adult passerby. Children in the first months of life may have a flattened occiput suggesting prolonged periods of unattended recumbency.

Older children often have educational problems and problems of school attendance. School attendance is not enforced and in some families children are deliberately kept off school. Children from such families are usually well known to the educational welfare department.

4. Protection and supervision

Failure to protect is a common sign of neglect. Many of these children have frequent attendances at the Casualty Department having ingested all manner of household products and medications. Parents pay scant attention to household safety often leaving hot irons and dangerous objects within reach of children. Lack of attention to safety together with an absence of common protective devices such as fire guards and stair guards predispose these children to accidents.

Supervision of young children is often inappropriately delegated to children a few years older. Children may be left in the home for long periods without any supervision. Other parents do not keep a check on the whereabouts of their young children, who are left to their own devices. Parents may take a baby to a public house, the child being left in a pram outside.

5. Shelter, clothing and warmth

As far as shelter is concerned it is difficult to define a minimal standard as many children come from impoverished families. The basic requisite of housing inhabited by young children is that it should be safe and of sufficient cleanliness so as not to constitute a health hazard. Neglectful parents sometimes lock children out of the home as a form of chastisement.

Clothing is often dirty and ill fitting. Socks and plastic pants may be supported by rubber bands which are too tight leaving marks after removal. Persistent exposure to cold causes chilblains (perniosis) of the extremities. In winter particularly, hands and feet may have a deep pink/purple colour and may appear oedematous. Glover has called this 'deprivation hands and feet'.

Children who are neglected are frequently abused as well. Neglected children should be carefully monitored for physical signs of abuse. The characteristics of parents who neglect their children are generally the same as those of parents who abuse children. These are discussed in Chapter 1, The epidemiology of child abuse.

'Failure to gain weight appropriately'

An editorial in the *Lancet* in 1990 suggested that this term be applied to children who fail to gain weight appropriately in response to inadequate calorie intake. It is a more apt description of the child's plight than the commonly used term 'failure to thrive'. It is usually a problem of children below three as older children make an effort to obtain food. In two-thirds of those receiving inadequate calories the reason is neglect. Sills refers to this group as having 'environmental deprivation' as the source of the blame should not focus on the mother alone but on the father, family members and the non-family support system. The commonly used term 'maternal deprivation' is invidious in such circumstances. A third do not gain weight because calorie intake is diminished on account of feeding difficulty ('accidental' neglect). Parents, usually out of ignorance, have misguided views about the quantity and type of food children require. Feeding techniques and preparation of formula may be faulty. Rarely, maternal milk supply is inadequate. In Britain insufficient calorie intake through parental poverty or deliberate starvation is very rare indeed.

What is 'appropriate' weight gain? It cannot be emphasised too strongly that children should always be weighed naked on accurate scales. In Britain weight measurements should be plotted on Gairdner Pearson (Castlemead Publications) or similar charts.

Maximum centile at four to eight weeks is a better predictor of centile at a year than birth weight, which is very much dependent on maternal and pregnancy related factors. Inappropriate weight gain would be downward deviation of centiles related to maximum centile at four to eight weeks. By definition 3% of children are normally below the third centile. For those below the third centile at four to eight weeks inappropriate weight gain would be any downward deviation.

When children are weighed accurate measurements of length and head circumference should be made. These are usually normal as length and head circumference are only affected when calorie deprivation is severe and prolonged.

Management

About 3–5% of children are admitted to hospital each year because of concern about their weight gain. The paediatrician has the task of deciding whether there may be a physical (organic) cause and which investigations, if any, should be undertaken. A detailed history with particular emphasis on the feeding and social history together with physical examination will distinguish the vast majority with an organic problem. Of those children admitted to hospital this group usually accounts for less than 20% and in most instances the diagnosis is arrived at with a few specific investigations.

Hospital admission has the great advantage of confirming the diagnosis of calorie deprivation and establishing whether the cause is a feeding problem or true neglect. In general where the diagnosis is true neglect mothers will not opt to stay on the ward with the child. When these mothers visit the ward their formula preparation, feeding technique and the way they relate to the child should be carefully reviewed. A period of less than two weeks is required to show accelerated weight gain where the diagnosis is calorie deprivation. A gain in weight of more than 50 grams a day where food is the only 'treatment' is highly suggestive.

Failure to gain weight due to 'accidental' neglect is usually remedied by close supervision and re-education. Such children can be monitored in the community by the health visitor. Where the cause is genuine neglect the outlook is far less encouraging and Social Services (or NSPCC) involvement is mandatory. In many such cases statutory action will be required.

Growth failure due to psychosocial deprivation

This is a well-known and common phenomenon. Both linear growth and weight do not realise their full potential as a result of psychosocial deprivation. These children have a transient impairment of growth hormone release. They are usually older than those who do not gain weight through calorie deprivation. Many, however, have a history of poor weight gain in infancy through neglect.

Clinical features may be similar to growth hormone deficiency, the social background helping to distinguish the two. Many have 'infantile body proportions', the legs being relatively shorter than the trunk. There is often a long history of disordered behaviour around food. Children may 'steal' food in the home or hoard it. Others gorge themselves until they vomit. Doctors should not be beguiled by the pretence of caring many parents give. Their hypercritical pejorative attitude creates a feeling of low self-esteem and outright rejection in the child. The response is to show his defiance by antisocial behaviour such as encopresis and enuresis.

Removal from the adverse environment is usually followed by a remarkable increase in both height and weight (see Figure 5.1). Rapid brain growth may even cause widening of cranial sutures. Growth changes are often accompanied by behaviour and personality changes, children becoming more outgoing and sociable. It cannot be stressed too strongly that the detection of this condition is urgent so that long-term damage can be avoided by placing the child in a nurturing environment.

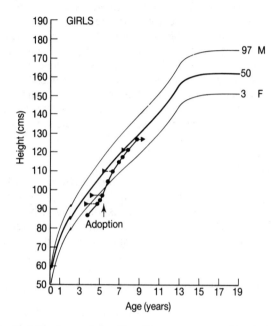

Figure 5.1 Height chart of Sophie. She was repeatedly abused and was happily adopted shortly after her fifth birthday. After adoption her height caught up with her bone age (▲) and mid-parental height (shown on right are her mother's height M, and father's height F). Her weight chart showed a similar pattern.

Further Reading

1. Altemeier WA et al. Antecedents of child abuse. *Journal of Pediatrics* 1982; **100**: 823–9.
2. Altemeier WA et al. Prospective study of antecedents for nonorganic failure to thrive. *Journal of Pediatrics* 1985; **106**: 360–5.
3. Ellerstein NS, Ostrov BE. Growth patterns in children hospitalised because of caloric-deprivation failure to thrive. *American Journal of Diseases of Children* 1985; **139**: 164–6.

 4. Neifert MR, Seacot JM, Jobe WE. Lactation failure due to insufficient glandular development of the breast. *Pediatrics* 1985; **76**: 823-8.
 5. Glover 5, Nicoll A, Pullan C. Deprivation hands and feet. *Archives of Disease in Childhood* 1985; **60**: 976-7.
 6. King JM, Taitz LS. Catch up growth following abuse. *Archives of Disease in Childhood* 1985; **60**: 1152-4.
 7. Helfer RE. The developmental basis of child abuse and neglect: an epidemiological approach. In: Helfer RE, Kempe RS eds. *The Battered Child*. Chicago: University of Chicago Press, 1987.
 8. Schmitt BD, Mauro RD. Nonorganic failure to thrive: an outpatient approach. *Child Abuse and Neglect* 1989; **13**: 235–48.
 9. Christoffel KK, Forsyth BWC. Mirror image of environmental deprivation: severe childhood obesity of psychological origin. *Child Abuse and Neglect* 1989; **13**: 249-56.
10. Skuse DH. Emotional abuse and delay in growth. In: Meadow R ed. *ABC of Child Abuse*. British Medical Journal Publications, 1989.
11. Anonymous. Failure to thrive revisited. *Lancet* 1990; **2**: 662–3.
12. Edwards AGK, Halse PC, Parkin JM, Waterston AJR. Recognising failure to thrive in early childhood. *Archives of Disease in Childhood* 1990; **65**: 1263–5.
13. Sills RH. Failure to thrive. In: Stockman JA ed. *Difficult Diagnosis in Pediatrics*. Philadelphia: WB Saunders, 1990.
14. Brayden RM et al. Antecedents of child neglect in the first 2 years of life. *Journal of Pediatrics* 1992; **120**: 426–9.
15. Wales JKH, Herber SM, Taitz LS. Height and body proportions in child abuse. *Archives of Disease in Childhood* 1992; **67**: 632–5.

6   Emotional abuse

It is not easy to disentangle emotional abuse from other forms of child abuse, emotional abuse frequently being inseparable as a specific entity. Unlike physical abuse, where the evidence is available for all to see, emotional abuse is often subtle and difficult to diagnose. Greater effort is required for its documentation for court purposes. The difficulty wi h diagnosis is probably reflected in the fact that in 1987 only 1% of children on the NSPCC register were in the category of emotional abuse. Like other forms of child maltreatment emotional abuse transcends the social spectrum but is heavily weighted at the bottom end.

Garbarino has referred to the emotionally abused child as 'psychologically battered'.[1] He has written that 'behaviour is considered psychologically abusive when it conveys a culture-specific message of rejection or impairs a socially relevant psychological process, such as the development of a coherent positive self concept'. He has defined five forms of 'psychically destructive' behaviour.

1. Rejecting – behaviours that communicate or constitute abandonment, such as showing no affection or not acknowledging the child's accomplishments. There are no positive remarks and, if the child does something praiseworthy, the parents merely make this an excuse for further criticism. A typical remark is 'you see, he can do it if he tries. The trouble is he never does.'
2. Isolating – the child is cut off from normal social experiences by the actions of the parent. He is prevented from forming friendships and is made to believe that he is alone in the world. 'Overprotective' parents who fail to send their children to school for a variety of trivial medical or sometimes no reasons fall into this category.
3. Ignoring – emotional and intellectual development is stifled by the child being deprived of stimulation.
4. Terrorising – threatening the child with vague or extreme punishment, creating a climate of unpredictability and the use of scare tactics. This is 'emotional' bullying.
5. Corrupting – the child is 'mis-socialised'; he is actively encouraged to engage in antisocial destructive behaviour, such deviant behaviour is reinforced.

A workable legal definition of emotional abuse is contained in the Child Welfare Act of the Canadian province of Alberta.[2] It states that a child is emotionally impaired (abused):

1. if there is substantial and observable impairment of the child's mental or emotional functioning that is evidenced by a mental or behavioural disorder, including anxiety, depression, withdrawal, aggression or delayed development, and
2. there are reasonable and probable grounds to believe that the emotional injury is the result of
   (a) rejection
   (b) deprivation of affection or cognitive stimulation
   (c) exposure to domestic violence or severe domestic disharmony, or
   (d) inappropriate criticism, threats, humiliation, accusations of or expectations towards the child, or
   (e) the mental or emotional condition of the guardian of the child or chronic alcohol or drug abuse by anyone living in the same residence as the child.

Emotional damage is probably the most devastating consequence of child maltreatment. While psychosocial growth impairment (see page 33) is another serious result of emotional abuse it is unusual. The vast majority of children with emotional abuse are of normal size. There are a number of studies which have examined the effects of child/emotional abuse on the mental development of the child. These have recently been reviewed by Goldson.[3] In general it can be concluded that some abused children display a variety of behavioural, emotional and physical symptoms, these being a subconscious 'cry for help'. The behaviour of the preschool child is often characterised by apathy and withdrawal and an inability to enjoy themselves (anhedonia). The child has a blank expression, 'frozen watchfulness' (see Figure 4.3), or exhibits gaze avoidance (see Figure 4.4) or smiles nonchalantly. Delay in development, particularly language, is common. There are often problems of attachment. Children are excessively clingy, at times even clinging to strangers. Studies show that in comparison with unabused children they are not only dependent but lack creativity and have a low self-esteem. Furthermore, aggression, impulsivity and distrust make for difficulty in forming relationships. These effects become even more striking as the child gets older. Conduct disorders are particularly common in school age children. Their poor socialisation makes them unpopular with peers and teachers. They are lacking in ambition, concentrate poorly and have a low academic achievement.

There are maltreated children who are unscathed by the experience, however a consensus of studies would suggest that some are profoundly affected. Many abused children have parents who were abused. These parents frequently exist in a state of poverty in poor housing with few material comforts. Generally they are unskilled, unemployed, often with a criminal record. Some have mental illness, personality disorder, educational subnormality. This is not the most propitious social background for nurturing children and begs the question, 'Are the deleterious emotional effects of child abuse a product of the child's socio-economic environment or the abuse *per se*?' While both probably contribute research would seem to suggest that the effect of the abnormal environment is the pre-eminent factor.

It is the potential long-term effects of child/emotional abuse that are the most worrying. It is not yet established which events and what circumstances are associated with the greatest risk of long-term problems. While some would argue that the evidence is not compelling, there is an impressive link between abuse in childhood and psychopathology in some adults. This in turn may be associated with relationships and/or sexual problems. In the case of sexual abuse it needs to be emphasised that the effects should not be exaggerated. Overstatement may cause further harm to the victims.

Another grave cause for concern is the frequent intergenerational continuity of child abuse in families. Between two-thirds and three-quarters of abusing parents report punitive upbringing, a rate well in excess of spouses/partners. Egeland studied the variables that distinguish mothers who broke the cycle of abuse from mothers who abused their own children.[4] Abused mothers who broke the cycle were significantly more likely to have received emotional support from a non-abusing adult during childhood, also they had received therapy at some time and had a non-abusive, stable, emotionally supportive and satisfying relationship with a mate. Abused mothers who re-enacted their maltreatment with their own children experienced significantly more life stress and were anxious, dependent, immature and depressed. The findings of this study have implications for the prevention of child abuse.

The management of abused children and their families is often a long and difficult process. It depends particularly on the presence and nature of any psychiatric disorder present in the parents or child, and more importantly the motivation of the parents to receive help. In many instances therapy will need to be initiated while the child is in care, or while a parent is facing criminal charges or is on probation. Separation of the child and parents may not be harmful if it is managed properly as part of a long-term plan of treatment and rehabilitation of the family. In most cases a number of agencies will also be involved such as the police, Social Services and probation. The interest of the child and family is best served by close co-operation and communication between the therapist (child psychiatrist/psychologist) and other professionals as part of a multidisciplinary approach.

Treatment needs to be aimed at the family and the child. Nicol compared two contrasting therapies for the treatment of child abuse; a focused casework approach for the whole family versus structured play therapy for the child.[5] In terms of outcome the former seemed to have the edge, but structured play therapy was helpful. Perhaps the ideal strategy would be to use both modalities simultaneously.

In this section on emotional abuse nothing has been said of peer related abuse. Bullying is widespread in all schools in Britain despite stringent efforts to stamp it out. Research has shown that bullying has a profound psychological effect on the victim and may impede educational performance. Children who are perceived as 'different' are frequently the victims of bullying. Examples are children of different race, religion or those with handicaps.

References

1. Garbarino J, Guttman E, Seeley JW. The Psychologically Battered Child. San Francisco: Jossey Bass, 1986.
2. Government of Alberta, Child Welfare Act. Edmonton: Queen's Printer, 1984.
3. Goldson E. The affective and cognitive sequelae of child maltreatment. *Pediatric Clinics of North America* 1991; **38**: 1481–96.
4. Egeland B, Jacobvitz B, Sroufe LA. Breaking the cycle of abuse. *Child Development* 1988; **59**: 1080–8.
5. Nicol A et al. A focused casework approach to the treatment of child abuse: a controlled comparison. *Journal of Child Psychology and Psychiatry* 1988; **5**: 703.
6. Lynch MA. The prognosis of child abuse. *Journal of Child Psychology and Psychiatry* 1978; **19**: 175–80.
7. Goensbauer TJ, Sands K. Distorted affective communication in abused/neglected infants and their potential impact on caretakers. *American Journal of Child Psychiatry* 1979; **18**: 236.
8. Taitz LS. Follow up of children 'at risk' of child abuse: effect of support on emotional and intellectual development. *Child Abuse and Neglect* 1981; **5**: 231–40.
9. Elmer E. Outcome of residential treatment for abused and high risk infants. *Child Abuse and Neglect* 1986; **10**: 351–60.
10. Mullen PE, Romans Clarkson SE, Walton VA, Herbison PG. Impact of sexual and physical abuse on women's mental health. *Lancet* 1988; **1**: 841–5.
11. Anonymous. Cycles of violence in child physical abuse. *Lancet* 1991; **338**: 88–9.
12. Creighton SJ, Noyes P. *Child abuse Trends in England and Wales 1983–1987*. London: National Society for the Prevention of Cruelty to Children, 1989.
13. Whitwell D. The significance of childhood sexual abuse for adult psychiatry. *British Journal of Hospital Medicine* 1990; **43**: 346–52.
14. Gomes-Schwartz B, Horowitz JM, Cordorelli AP. *Child Sexual Abuse: The Initial Effects*. London: Sage Publications, 1990.

15. Sheldrick C. Adult sequelae of child sexual abuse. *British Journal of Psychiatry* (Supplement 10) 1991; **158**: 55–62.
16. Palmer RL. Effects of childhood sexual abuse on adult mental health. *British Journal of Hospital Medicine* 1992; **48**: 9–10.
17. O'Hagan K. *Emotional And Psychological Abuse Of Children*. Buckingham: Open University Press, 1993.

7 Bruising injuries to skin and subcutaneous tissues

Bruising is the commonest injury in child abuse. Any bruising in a child below nine months should be viewed with suspicion. After that age the frequency of accidental bruising increases gradually to reach a plateau at about three years.

What is a bruise?

A bruise is an injury to the skin and subcutaneous tissues causing rupture of the capillaries and small blood vessels with extravasation of blood. The time interval between the injury and the appearance of colour change is determined both by the force and by the site of impact. In superficial tissue injury the extravasated blood produces colour change relatively quickly, most rapid bruising appearing in loose vascular tissue such as that around the orbit. In deep tissue injury leaked blood takes the line of least resistance tracking between fascial or muscle planes to become apparent several hours or days later, sometimes at a site different from impact. For instance a deep tissue injury to the upper thigh may produce a bruise above the knee a day or two later.

Doctors are frequently asked by courts, police and social workers to express an opinion about the force required to inflict bruising. Owing to the wide variation in 'bruisability' between individuals the answer cannot be precise and should be qualified. Site is an important consideration, lax vascular tissues such as those around the eye or scrotum require less force.

When faced with a child with bruising the following features distinguish accidental bruising from abuse:

1. location of bruising,
2. pattern of bruising,
3. number of bruises, and
4. dating of bruises.

Location

Table 7.1 shows the location of accidental and abusive injuries. Some

Table 7.1   The common sites of accidental and inflicted bruising.

Accidental	Inflicted
Forehead	Ears and sides of face
Under chin	Neck
Spinal prominences	Trunk
Hips (iliac crests)	Proximal arms
Distal arms	Thighs
Shins	Buttocks
	Genitalia

overlap is inevitable but in general accidental injuries involve skin over bony prominences. For example it would be quite normal for an active toddler to have bruising of the forehead, bony areas of face and chin. About a quarter of children below age ten will have some bruising on the shins. Bruising on the arms, particularly the upper part, trunk and thighs, is usually caused by finger marks as a result of the child having been gripped. Falls down stairs cause facial and distal limb bruising. Chastisement with a hand or implement accounts for most bruising of the buttocks, lower back and lateral thighs.

Bruising of the side of the face is a common site of an inflicted injury (Figure 7.1), the pressure from the fingers causes capillary disruption at the edges giving the characteristic pattern. Bruising of the upper lip and labium frenulum (sometimes with a tear) may be caused by a bottle or dummy being forced into the mouth or by a blow (Figure 10.4). Bruising of ears and the neck is rarely accidental. Ear bruising is due to the ears being boxed, pulled or pinched. Unlike the ear which is boxed, pulling and pinching causes bruising on both sides of the lobe. Neck bruising is due to the neck being gripped in an attempt to throttle the child or to lift or restrain him. Children may be gripped by the neck as the head is banged against a wall. Rarely a circumferential area of bruising will be seen as a result of something being tied around the neck in an attempt to strangle the child.

Black eyes (periorbital haematomas) are frequently seen in inflicted injuries of the face. The object inflicting the injury (for example a fist) will usually be sufficiently large to avoid causing trauma to the eye but will damage the capillaries in the tissues surrounding the eye. The tissues about the eye are fragile requiring little trauma to induce bleeding. There may be a slow, persistent ooze in which case the bruising is most prominent a day or two later. Bilateral black eyes can occur as a result of a bump on the forehead or head; the blood in the subaponeurotic space tracks down to the tissues about the orbit (see Figure 7.2). There is often no bruising at the site of impact and the bruising about the eyes becomes apparent after some hours. Unlike injury about the eye these black eyes will not be swollen or tender. 'Allergic shiners', which occur in allergic rhinitis, have on occasion been confused with black eyes. The blue/black coloration in the 'allergic shiner' is due to vascular congestion in the periorbital tissues.

Purpura or petechia (pin point haemorrhages) can arise from capillary disruption at any site due to pressure from squeezing or other forms of skin trauma. These can also occur spontaneously from a sudden increase in intrathoracic pressure as occurs with vigorous coughing, vomiting or crying. When this happens they are usually situated on the chest or neck but can be found in the mouth and conjunctiva.

The pattern (configuration)

The pattern of the marks helps distinguish accidental from abusive injuries. For example striking with a looped cord produces characteristic loops (Figure 7.3). Children are frequently hit with belts, sticks, shoes, etc. which produce characteristic imprints. Hand marks vary considerably depending on the way the skin is injured. The marks from such actions as grabbing, slapping (Figure 7.1), pinching, poking

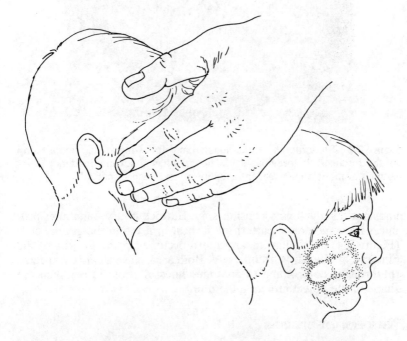

Figure 7.1 Typical facial slap bruise. Finger pressure causes capillary disruption and bleeding at the edges creating a silhouette of parallel lines.

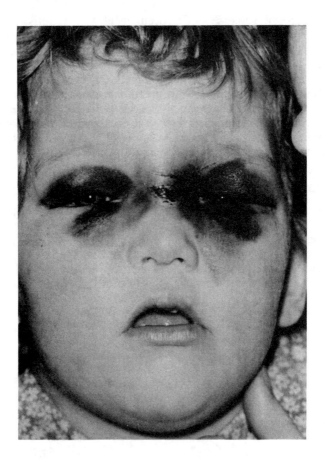

Figure 7.2 Bilateral periorbital haematomas following an accidental bump on the forehead the previous day. The child has a bleeding tendency (idiopathic thrombocytopaenia). Inflicted injury had been suspected.

and squeezing will vary considerably. Buttock injury sometimes produces a characteristic pattern of vertical bruising in the gluteal cleft (Figure 7.4). A similar linear pattern occurs over the top rim of the pinna when the ear is traumatised. Both areas have a convex surface, the bruising conforming to anatomic lines of stress rather than the shape of the object inflicting the injury.

Number of bruises

While a large number of bruises might raise suspicion of non-accidental injury it should be borne in mind that the converse is not

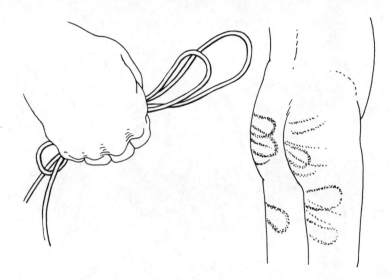

Figure 7.3   Looped bruising inflicted with an electric flex.

true. Non-accidental fractures of the skull, limbs and ribs can occur with no apparent bruising. It is often very difficult to decide when bruising is 'excessive' given the range of activity of young children. There can be little doubt that some children are accident prone and will have frequent bruises. The number of bruises should be viewed both in the context of activity level and in the explanation provided. For example extensive bruising on the face and distal limbs of a toddler would be plausible given a history of a fall down stairs, but not a fall in snow. There are rare reports of extensive bruising being associated with rhabdomyolysis and myoglobinuria; the muscle damage from a severe beating causing severe pain, weakness and a risk of renal failure.

When confronted with a child with excessive bruises or who appears to bruise easily, the possibility of a bleeding disorder should be excluded. Most children with a bleeding disorder will have a history of frequent bruising, nose or joint bleeds since the first months of life. It also becomes necessary to exclude a bleeding disorder when a parent alleges 'easy bruisability', particularly when the bruising is non-specific and the case is likely to go to litigation. Imprint mark bruising and bruising the cause of which is not denied do not require investigation. Tests to exclude a bleeding disorder in suspected non-accidental injury are shown in Table 7.2. A bleeding time is mandatory to exclude abnormalities of blood vessels and

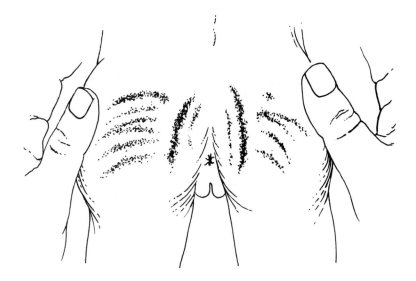

Figure 7.4   Parted buttocks of girl who was spanked on both buttocks. Note some horizontal finger mark bruising and typical vertical bruising in the gluteal clefts.

Table 7.2   Tests which are required to exclude a bleeding disorder in suspected non-accidental injury.

1.   Full blood count, film
2.   Platelet – count, size and shape
3.   Partial thromboplastin time
4.   Prothrombin time
5.   Thrombin time
6.   Factor XIII assay
7.   Fibrinogen
8.   Bleeding time

qualitative platelet defects. A bleeding diathesis in such cases is likely to be missed if only coagulation studies are undertaken as these are usually normal. It should be borne in mind that a bleeding diathesis and non-accidental injury are not mutually exclusive; a child with a bleeding tendency could be non-accidentally injured.

It is important that the bleeding screen be done shortly after the bruising was sustained. Some children with viral infections temporarily develop circulating anticoagulants which cause abnormal tests only to correct spontaneously a few days later. Questions should also be asked about concurrent drug usage as certain drugs may interfere with platelet function.

Dating of bruises

Abused children often have a number of bruises of varying age. The colour of a bruise is sometimes of importance from the medico-legal point of view in determining the age of an injury. It should always be emphasised that the use of colour to date bruises is very imprecise. Bruises of identical age and cause on the same part of the body may not show the same colours nor undergo changes at an identical rate. When assessing colour confounding variables include factors such as lighting and individual colour perception. The colour and duration of the bruise depend on the amount of blood extravasated and the distance from the skin surface. Table 7.3 is a guide showing the sequential changes in dating a bruise.

Table 7.3 The dating of bruises.

0–2 days	swollen and tender
0–5 days	red/blue/purple
> 5 days	evolves through a sequential pattern – green/yellow/brown
1–4 weeks	resolves

Pseudobruises

In non-Caucasian races dark blue/grey spots (Mongolian spots) are often present on the back, buttocks and extensor surface of limbs in the first years of life. Such spots may be confused with bruising. Other skin conditions which look like bruises and may be mistaken for non-accidental injury are erythema nodosum, anaphylactoid purpura and phytodermatitis. Ink, paint and blue dye from clothing such as jeans may simulate bruising.

Bite marks

These are usually two crescentic marks which in some cases will be joined to give a circular appearance (see Figure 7.5). The appearance is dependent on the pressure exerted and its duration, and the tightness of the skin. For example a bite on the breast will look different from a bite on the back where the skin is tight. Initially teeth marks are pale, the capillaries at their edge become stretched and damaged creating a crescentic/circular bruise. Immediately afterwards it may

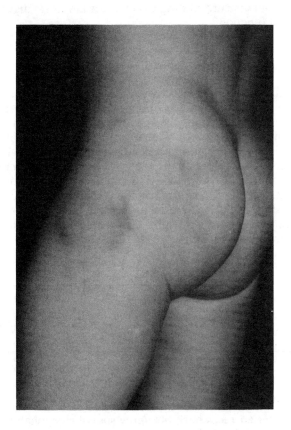

Figure 7.5   The crescentic/circular bruising of a human bite mark.

be swollen and stiff but with resolution of swelling the skin moves causing an alteration of the pattern. The centre of the bite may contain a bruised area caused by negative pressure from sucking on the skin or by positive pressure from the tongue pushing on the skin.

Bruising from a bite is always non-accidental. Children commonly bite each other. When encountering a child with bite marks it is often necessary to determine whether these were inflicted by an adult or a child. A line drawn between the mid point of the canines (third tooth on each side) can be used as a guide to distinguish primary from secondary dentition. A distance of less than 3 cm suggests primary dentition (less than eight years). Guidance can be obtained from the work of Moorees by measuring arch width and cumulative widths of the six upper front and six lower front teeth (four incisors and two canines respectively). The mean difference between the arches of a five year old and an adult is 4.4 mm (maxilla) and 2.5 mm (mandible). The mean cumulative width difference between deciduous and permanent teeth is 10 mm (upper) and 7 mm (lower). Precise identification requires a forensic dentist to make an impression of the teeth of the alleged perpetrator for comparison with photographs which will need to be repeated in order to obtain the best definition of the mark.

Human bites differ from animal bites in that the size of the mark is generally smaller and the arch narrower. The animal incisors cause the skin to be ripped rather than crushed. The skin from a severe animal bite where the skin is extensively torn gives the impression of a surgical wound.

Further reading

1. Moorees CFA. *The Dentitian of the Growing Child*. Boston: Harvard University Press, 1959.
2. Wilson EF. Estimation of age of cutaneous contusions. *Pediatrics* 1977; **60**: 750.
3. Pascoe JM et al. Patterns of skin injury in non-accidental and accidental injury. *Pediatrics* 1979; **64**: 245.
4. Roberton DM, Barbor P, Hull D. Unusual injury? Recent injury in normal children and children with suspected non accidental injury. *British Medical Journal* 1982; **285**: 1399.
5. Levine LJ. Bite marks in child abuse. In: Sanger RG and Bross DC eds. *Clinical Management of Child Abuse and Neglect: A Guide for the Dental Professional*. Chicago: Quintessence Publishing, 1984.
6. O'Hare AE, Eden OB. Bleeding disorders and non-accidental injury. *Archives of Disease in Childhood* 1984; **59**: 860–4.
7. Schwengel D, Ludwig S. Rhabdomyolysis and myoglobinuria as manifestations of child abuse. *Pediatric Emergency Care* 1985; **1**: 194.
8. Joffe M, Ludwig S. Stairway injuries in children. *Pediatrics* 1988; **82**: 457.
9. Wheeler DM, Hobbs CJ. Mistakes in diagnosing non-accidental injury: 10 years' experience. *British Medical Journal* 1988; **296**: 1233.
10. Gold MH, Roenigh HH, Smith ES, Pierce LJ. Human bite marks. *Clinical Pediatrics* 1989; **28**: 329–31.
11. Langlois NEI, Gresham GA. The ageing of bruises: a review and study of the colour changes with time. *Forensic Science International* 1991; **50**: 227–38.
12. Lanter RR, Ros SP. Blue jean thighs. *Pediatrics* 1991; **88**: 417.
13. Feldman KW. Patterned abusive bruises of the buttocks and pinnae. *Pediatrics* 1992; **90**: 633–6.

8 Head injuries

Head injury accounts for more disability and death than any other type of non-accidental injury.

Scalp bruising is often difficult to detect. Tissue swelling or tenderness may draw attention to it. Unlike bruising, swelling is more apparent, but may sometimes only be noticed as a widening of soft tissues on x-ray. Any trauma to the scalp can cause a subaponeurotic (subgaleal) haemorrhage which is apparent as a boggy scalp swelling. Lifting a child by the hair or pulling forcefully, particularly on a ponytail or plaits, can induce a subaponeurotic bleed.

Traumatic alopecia (see Figure 8.1) results from a forceful pull on the child's hair. This can easily be differentiated from other forms of alopecia in that the outline of the bald patches is irregular. The

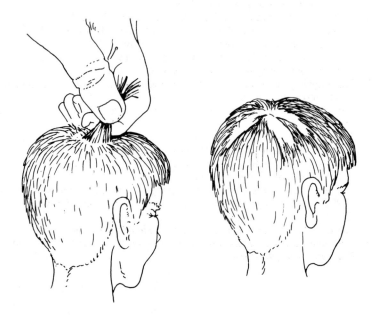

Figure 8.1 Traumatic alopecia from hair-pulling.

scalp may be tender with petechial haemorrhages at the hair roots if traction has been recent.

Injuries of the head are of two types: impact or shaking, sometimes both. The morbidity and mortality are related to the extent of cerebral contusion and not the mechanism of injury. Areas of architectural disruption, haemorrhage and oedema may be localised or generalised. In the acute phase the raised intracranial pressure associated with brain swelling may be life threatening, requiring urgent treatment. Areas of brain become infarcted and atrophied. In children who survive some make a complete recovery, others are left with a spectrum of neurological abnormalities and seizures.

Impact injuries

These occur when the head is banged by or against a hard object. The impact causes craniocerebral distortion causing the skull to fracture along stress lines. The fracture may be linear or the skull may 'burst' with tearing of the meninges and wide separation of the fragments (see Figure 8.2). It should be noted that fractures can occur away from the point of impact and that fractures frequently occur without bruising. It is common to find soft tissue swelling over the site of the fracture, this often developing a day or two after the incident.

Accidental skull fractures are common in early childhood. Children are dropped or fall in the home. When faced with a young child with a skull fracture it is the task of the interviewing doctor to judge whether the history is compatible with the degree of injury. Some guidance may be obtained from studies by Hobbs, Meservy, and Leventhal. Meservy and Leventhal have shown that most accidental and inflicted injuries cause single linear fractures involving one parietal bone. If both parietal bones or a parietal bone and another are fractured the likelihood of an inflicted injury increases. Hobbs has indicated that fractures of the occipital bone are seldom accidental and should always arouse suspicion of abuse. However, in the Leventhal study 10% of accidental fractures were occipital.

Most accidental and inflicted fractures are narrow and referred to as 'hairline' being 1-2 mm in width. According to Hobbs a width of more than 3 mm ('diastatic') or a 'growing' fracture strongly suggest abuse. When the skull 'bursts' (see Figure 8.2) the brain and meninges evaginate between the edges of the fracture preventing healing and causing the fracture to 'grow'. The evagination is also known as a leptomeningeal cyst and eventually requires surgical correction.

Complex fractures are more often inflicted than accidental. It should however be noted that in a study by Leventhal short distance falls between 60 and 120 cm caused complex fractures. Complex is defined as two or more distinct fractures of any type or a single fracture with multiple components. The latter includes a branched

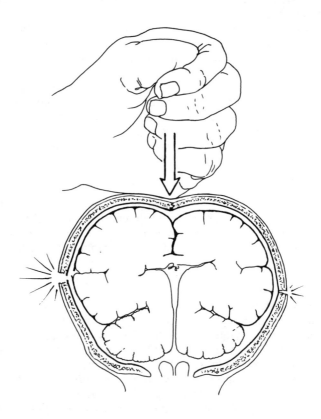

Figure 8.2 Skull distortion and fractures caused by a blow to the head. On the left can be seen bone separation with a tear of the meninges. On the right is a linear fracture.

linear fracture. Leventhal, unlike Hobbs and Meservy, also classified depressed and wide ('diastatic') fractures as complex.

Accidental, depressed fractures are well localised and would be consistent with the head having struck a projection of some sort. Such fractures would be inconsistent with a fall on a flat object. Inflicted areas of depression are often many and extensive and usually have multiple components.

Intracranial injury is exceedingly rare after a simple fall. Any child with loss of consciousness after a 'fall' should arouse suspicion of non-accidental injury. It cannot be emphasised too strongly that these points of differentiation are a guide, each incident requiring careful evaluation of the degree of trauma in relation to the radiological changes. There are no skull x-ray changes specific for abuse. When evaluating the studies the study population should be considered. The Hobbs study represents the extreme end of the spectrum with 19 out of 29 being fatalities.

The question of fall distance frequently arises in medico-legal work. Doctors presenting medical evidence would be well advised to familiarise themselves with the literature on the subject. When children fall accidentally the severity of the injury is dependent on the distance and hardness of the floor surface. From studies in the literature, which are based on reports of parents about minor falls or documented falls of children in hospital, it can be concluded that children falling short distances seldom sustain a skull fracture. The risk of a fall of less than 90 cm (3 feet) being associated with a skull fracture is probably less than 2%. In a five year study of fractures in children under three Leventhal identified eight children with linear parietal fractures after falls of less than 60 cm, bed or sofa height.

Basilar skull fracture may not be apparent on x-ray, but certain clinical features point to such a fracture. These are bruising behind the ear (over mastoid) known as a Battle's sign or bilateral bruising of the eyelids. Such bruising can also occur after bleeding into the deep layers of the scalp; blood tracking downwards to these points of scalp attachment. Discharge of cerebrospinal fluid from the ear or nose indicates a communicating basal fracture.

'How old is the fracture?' is a question frequently asked of the expert witness. It is not possible to date skull fractures reliably. The presence of an overlying haematoma or soft tissue swelling indicates recent injury (0-10 days), but absence of these changes does not indicate old injury. Blurring of the fracture edges does indicate ageing of at least two weeks but is no help beyond that.

When skull fractures are detected in the first months of life cognisance should be given to the fact that they may have occurred at birth. Some depressed fractures occur *in utero*. Another source of confusion might be a cephalohaematoma (a subperiosteal haemorrhage) which may not be apparent immediately after birth but develops over a few days and may persist for two to three months. It is a fluctuant swelling over the parietal bone and is localised to suture lines.

Shaking injuries

Children who are shaken violently in a fit of temper are at risk of developing intracranial haemorrhage. These children, who are usually less than a year, are frequently thrown down onto the cot or bed after the episode of shaking. The fact that a skull fracture is an unusual accompaniment of an intracranial haemorrhage is probably a reflection of the soft surface with which they impact. Shaking injury is discussed in Chapter 9, Shaken Baby Syndrome.

Further reading

1. Kravitz H, Driessen G, Gomberg R, Korach A. Accidental falls from elevated surfaces in infants from birth to one year of age. *Pediatrics* 1969; **44**: Suppl: 869–76.
2. Helfer RE, Slovis TL, Black M. Injuries resulting when small children fall out of bed. *Pediatrics* 1977; **60**: 533–5.
3. Hobbs CJ. Skull fracture and the diagnosis of abuse. *Archives of Disease in Childhood* 1984; **59**: 246–52.
4. Billmire ME, Myers PA. Serious head injury in infants: accident or abuse? *Pediatrics* 1985; **75**: 340–2.
5. Nimityonskul P, Anderson LD. The likelihood of injuries when children fall out of bed. *Journal of Pediatric Orthopedics* 1987; **7**: 184.
6. Meservy CJ et al. Radiographic characteristics of skull fractures resulting from child abuse. *American Journal of Roentgenology* 1987; **149**: 173–5.
7. Kleinman PK et al. Radiologic contributions to the investigation and prosecution of cases of fatal infant abuse. *New England Journal of Medicine* 1989; **320**: 507–8.
8. Bruce DA. Head injuries in the pediatric population. *Current Problems in Pediatrics* 1990, volume 20, number 2.
9. Haller JO et al. Diagnostic imaging of child abuse. *Pediatrics* 1991; **87**: 262–4.
10. Williams RA. Injuries in infants and small children resulting from witnessed and corroborated free falls. *The Journal of Trauma* 1991; **31**: 1350–2.
11. Duhaime AC et al. Head injury in very young children: mechanisms, injury types, and ophthalmologic findings in 100 hospitalized patients younger than 2 years of age. *Pediatrics* 1992; **90**; 179–85.
12. Leventhal JM, Thomas SA, Rosenfield NS, Markowitz RI. Fractures in young children. Distinguishing child abuse from unintentional injuries. *American Journal of Diseases in Childhood* 1993; **147**: 87–92.
13. Lyons TJ, Oates RK. Falling out of bed: a relatively benign occurrence. *Pediatrics* 1993; **92**: 125–127.

9   Shaken Baby Syndrome

The Shaken Baby Syndrome is a well-recognised and common form of child abuse with a high mortality and morbidity. Shaking a baby as a form of chastisement is widespread and is thought by some to be socially acceptable. The main features of the syndrome are subdural and retinal haemorrhages caused by shaking. The vast majority of children with shaking injury are under 12 months.

What we now know about this syndrome owes much to an American radiologist, John Caffey. He proposed the name 'Whiplash Shaken Infant Syndrome' and pointed out that a reliable history is frequently absent, the diagnosis being made by a combination of physical, radiological and pathological evidence.

Shaking injuries usually occur in a sudden fit of rage often in response to a child who is crying uncontrollably. The child is violently shaken (see Figure 9.1) and the rapid acceleration/deceleration produces differential motion between the skull and its contents. Infants are particularly vulnerable to whiplash injury as the bridging cerebral veins (see Figure 9.2) are poorly supported as they pass through the subdural space. The to and fro motion of the brain causes traction and shearing of the veins. The pressure in the venous system is low in which case symptoms and signs may not be immediate but are apparent within 12 hours. Children usually present with loss of consciousness and/or seizures. There may be a preceding period of irritability. Suture separation and a bulging fontanelle indicate raised intracranial pressure. On most occasions infants who are shaken in a rage are not laid back gently in the crib but are thrown down sustaining an impact injury as well. When there is no evidence of impact injury or physical abuse and shaking is not admitted the diagnosis could be delayed. Most infants who have been shaken do not have a skull fracture. Rib fractures are sometimes caused by grasping of the chest during the shaking process.

On rare occasions vertebral abnormalities are sustained. These are in the lower thoracic/upper lumbar part of the spine and are caused by hyperextension/flexion as the head is tossed backwards and forwards. Characteristically there is narrowing of the disc space with notching of the anterior vertebral borders (see Figure 9.3). Only the most severe abnormalities are accompanied by damage to the spinal cord.

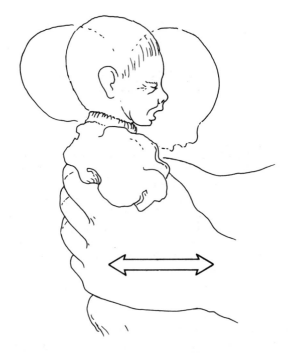

Figure 9.1   Whiplashing of the infant head caused by shaking.

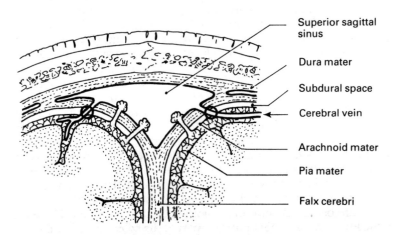

Figure 9.2   The site of rupture (◯) of the bridging cerebral veins in the subdural space. Bleeding arises from rupture of cerebral veins in the subdural space; a collection of blood extends over the frontal lobes. There may be a bulging fontanelle, convulsions and often retinal haemorrhages.

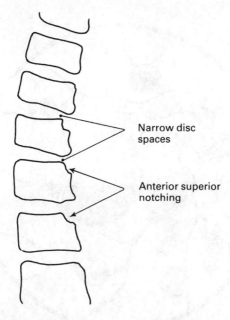

Figure 9.3 Typical vertebral changes in the Shaken Baby Syndrome. Changes are caused by hyperextension/flexion.

Most children with Shaken Baby Syndrome have retinal haemorrhages. The eye of the infant, like the brain, has certain anatomical features which predispose it to the noxious effect of whiplash injury. The vitreous is relatively solid and is tightly adherent to the lens and the retina especially around the macula. Shaking of the head causes the heavy lens to move rapidly backwards and forwards in the occular fluid; retinal traction causing small blood vessel disruption and haemorrhage at the point of firmest attachment around the macula (see Figure 9.4). Although intravascular pressure changes, resulting from increased cerebral or intrathoracic pressure, may contribute to the retinal haemorrhage, the primary cause is purported to be oscillation of the lens (see Figure 9.5).

While retinal haemorrhages are not pathognomonic of shaking, concentration of haemorrhage in the macula and surrounding area is very suggestive. Other causes of retinal haemorrhage are shown in Table 9.1.

When retinal haemorrhages are detected it may be difficult to time the injury. Most retinal haemorrhages resolve within a week or two. Massive blood accumulation would suggest a recent injury. This is particularly the case when an initial examination reveals retinal haemorrhage only and subsequent examination shows migration of blood

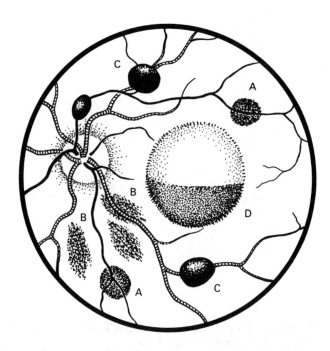

Figure 9.4 Retinal haemorrhage caused by shaking. Haemorrhage can occur at various anatomic sites. A, Dot or blot intraretinal haemorrhage. Note haemorrhage is behind the blood vessels. B, Flame-shaped superficial nerve fibre layer haemorrhage. C, Preretinal haemorrhage. Note haemorrhage is in front of blood vessels. D, Splitting of the retina (retinoschisis) in area of macula showing an elevated surface and a haemorrhagic fluid level in the ensuing cavity.

Table 9.1 Differential diagnosis of retinal haemorrhage in infants

Shaking injury
Chest compression – cardiac resuscitation; chest compression during vaginal delivery
Intracranial haemorrhage – may be spontaneous, accidental and non-accidental

Severe hypertension
Bleeding tendency (haemorrhagic diathesis)
Infection – generalised sepsis, meningitis, encephalitis, endocarditis, viral retinitis.

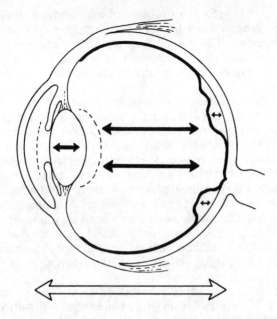

Figure 9.5 The mechanism of retinal haemorrhage in whiplash injury. The heavy lens oscillates in the ocular fluid transmitting the force through the vitreous to the retina.

into the vitreous. Sparse haemorrhage at the initial examination is consistent with both early or late injury, irrespective of the degree of trauma. As a general rule preservation of the pupillary light reflex is a good prognostic sign.

Not all shaking injuries are abusive. A young child with apnoea, a seizure or following an accident may be unintentionally violently shaken in a panic attempt to revive the child. If the child is not fully conscious the muscular hypotonia makes him particularly vulnerable to retinal and brain haemorrhage. The history in such a situation is of vital importance in ascertaining whether the shaking was abusive.

Adults who abusively shake children may invoke shaking as part of a resuscitative procedure in their defence. They may claim that the child was shaken after he was found apnoeic or with a seizure. In these instances skeletal survey is invaluable in sometimes highlighting evidence of abuse which would serve to negate the defence. This is particularly so in children who die when the charge is likely to be murder or manslaughter. A skeletal survey might reveal subtle x-ray changes such as metaphyseal chip fractures which are specific to abuse. Such changes would not be readily apparent on postmortem examination thereby depriving the Crown of valuable incriminating evidence and risking further exposure of any siblings to shaking.

Mydriatic drops should be used with extreme care when shake injury is supected. The use of short acting mydrilates such as 1% cyclopentolate may mask important neurological signs. If drops are used the pre-dilated size and reactivity of the pupil should be documented.

What is a chronic subdural haematoma? It is a subdural haematoma detected in infancy, the child usually presenting with one or more of the following: accelerated head growth, seizures, sporadic vomiting and failure to thrive. In the past these were frequently attributed to persisting birth trauma or were said to be 'spontaneous'. Both causes would now be viewed with scepticism. Subdural haemorrhage resulting from birth trauma usually presents in the first 24 hours. For it not to present in this way would be most unusual. It is now thought that many of the so called 'spontaneous' subdurals may have been caused by chronic shaking. The answer to the vexed question of what causes chronic subdurals should become evident with more frequent use of nuclear magnetic imaging (NMI). It has the ability to delineate areas of previous brain injury.

All children with a suspected subdural should have a computed tomographic (CT) scan. In most instances this will suffice but on occasion NMI will be required to delineate the abnormality further. Although ultrasonography may reveal intracranial abnormalities it is inadequate to exclude or fully evaluate intracranial injury. CT scan is easier to perform in the unstable patient and is better at detecting skull injuries and subarachnoid haemorrhage than NMI. The main advantage of NMI is that it is substantially more sensitive in identifying and characterising most intracranial sequelae of inflicted head injuries. Furthermore, it is better able to determine the age of extracerebral fluid collections.

It is frequent for shaken children with subdurals but without physical evidence of abuse to be diagnosed as having a metabolic problem, encephalitis/meningitis or a 'near miss' cot death also called acute life threatening event (ALTE). The perpetrator is unlikely to volunteer information in which case there may be a time lapse of hours (or days) before the correct diagnosis is arrived at. As soon as a subdural haemorrhage is suspected the expert opinion of a neurosurgeon should be obtained.

Further reading

1.   Caffey J. Multiple fractures of the long bones of infants suffering from subdural haematoma. American Journal of Roentgenology 1946; **56**: 163.
2.   Caffey J. On the theory and practice of shaking infants. American Journal of Diseases in Childhood 1972; **124**: 161–70.

3. Caffey J. The whiplash shaken infant syndrome. Manual shaking by the extremities with whiplash-induced intracranial and intraocular bleedings, linked with permanent brain damage and mental retardation. *Pediatrics* 1974; **54**: 396–403.

4. Kanter RK. Retinal haemorrhage after cardiopulmonary resuscitation in children: an etiologic reevaluation. *Journal of Pediatrics* 1986; **108**: 430–2.

5. Duhaime AC et al. The Shaken Baby Syndrome: a clinical, pathological and biomechanical study. *Journal of Neurosurgery* 1987; **66**: 409–15.

6. Newton R. Intracranial haemorrhage and non-accidental injury. *Archives of Diseases in Childhood* 1989; **64**: 188–90.

7. Alexander R et al. Serial abuse in children who are shaken. *American Journal of Diseases in Childhood* 1990; **144**: 58–60.

8. Alexander R, Sato Y, Smith W, Bennett T. Incidence of impact trauma with cranial injuries ascribed to shaking. *American Journal of Diseases in Childhood* 1990; **144**: 724–6.

9. Levin AV. Ocular manifestations of child abuse. *Ophthalmology Clinics of North America* 1990; **3**: 249–64.

10. Greenwald MJ. The Shaken Baby Syndrome. *Seminars in Ophthalmology* 1990; **5**: 202–15.

11. Goetting MG, Sowa B. Retinal hemorrhage after cardiopulmonary resuscitation in children: an etiologic reevaluation. *Pediatrics* 1990; **85**: 585–8.

12. Haller JO et al. Diagnostic imaging of child abuse. *Pediatrics* 1991; **87**: 262–4.

13. Smith WL et al. Magnetic resonance imaging evaluation of neonates with retinal hemorrhages. *Pediatrics* 1992; **89**: 332–3.

14. Duhaime AC. Head injury in very young children: mechanisms, injury types and ophthalmologic findings in 100 hospitalised patients younger than 2 years of age. *Pediatrics* 1992; **90**: 179–85.

10   Injuries of the face

Eye injuries

Injuries of the soft tissues about the eye are readily apparent as periorbital haematomas sometimes with swelling and tenderness. These 'black eyes', which are common, are frequently caused by a blow across the side of the face.

Inflicted injuries of the eye itself are not common but when they do occur morbidity is high, loss of sight often ensuing. When these injuries occur the advice of an ophthalmic consultant is invaluable. The most common injuries are intra-orbital haemorrhages (mainly retinal), periorbital and conjunctival haemorrhages, retinal detachment and tears (dialysis). Corneal injury, lens dislocation, and any other eye injury may be caused by child abuse (see Figure 10.1). If a red eye is apparent after trauma an examination under anaesthesia should be performed so that the intra-ocular pressure can be measured and the globe carefully inspected for rupture or perforation.

Accidental injury of the eye or its surrounding tissue is usually unilateral; bilateral eye injury should strongly raise suspicion of non-accidental injury (see Figure 10.2). However, it should be noted that bilateral ecchymoses may occur after a bump on the head or in association with a basal skull fracture, often a day or two after the incident. Subconjunctival haemorrhages are caused by direct trauma but can evolve spontaneously particularly following a valsalva manoeuvre* associated with vigorous coughing, retching or crying. Subconjunctival haemorrhage is normal in the newborn.

There is a spectrum of corneal injuries. The corneal epithelium may be abraded by contact producing a characteristic stain with fluorescein. Sharp objects produce deeper injuries. When such injuries are found in association with eyelid bruising, inflicted injury should be suspected. There are a number of reports of corneal damage caused by chemicals instilled in the eye. Corneal injuries rarely occur with

---

*Expiration against a closed glottis causing an increase in intrathoracic pressure.

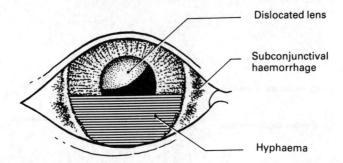

Figure 10.1 Eye injuries associated with child abuse.

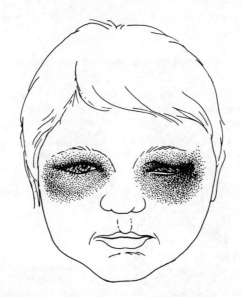

Figure 10.2 Bilateral periorbital haematomas. Such injuries should raise suspicion of non-accidental injury, but can occur accidentally.

forceps deliveries and are apparent in the first weeks of life.

The eye may be injured in two ways:

(a) *Direct trauma* (see Figure 10.3). Sudden compression of the front of the eye causes the pressure to be transmitted through the compartments of the eye. The fluid filling the chambers is forced peripherally and backwards causing distortion of the globe, structural damage and

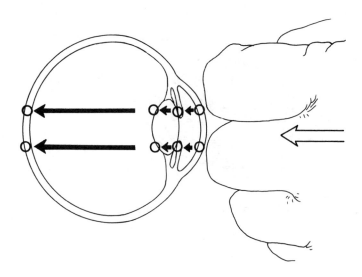

Figure 10.3   The transmission of a blunt force through the compartments of the eye.

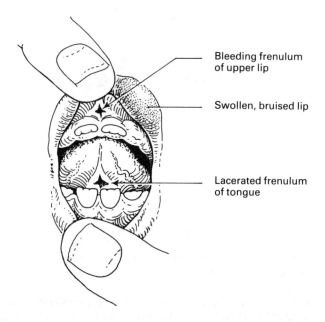

Bleeding frenulum
of upper lip

Swollen, bruised lip

Lacerated frenulum
of tongue

Figure 10.4   Common mouth injuries resulting from forced feeding. Injuries of the upper lip frenulum are most common.

haemorrhage. Haemorrhage in the anterior chamber (hyphema) may be readily apparent as a collection of blood with a fluid level in front of the iris (see Figure 10.1).

(b) *Shaking* Vigorous shaking causes acceleration/deceleration forces which are thought to damage the eye directly. In infancy the eye, like the brain, has certain anatomical features that seem likely to potentiate the noxious effect of whiplash injury. Shaking injury is discussed in Chapter 9, Shaken Baby Syndrome.

Mouth injuries

Common injuries around the mouth are bruising and laceration of the lips and tearing of a lingual or labial frenulum (see Figure 10.4). Teeth may be broken or avulsed and gums injured. Rarely the tongue may be lacerated as a result of a blow to the mandible and the mandible may be fractured.

Lips are injured by the force of a blunt object (usually a hand) trapping the lip between the object and the teeth. The sharp edge of the tooth may cause a laceration or contusion on the inside of the lip. Some lip injuries are accompanied by a torn frenulum. Lip injuries, whether contusions or lacerations, are not serious and look much worse than they actually are. The vast majority heal without treatment.

A frenulum tear of the lip or tongue in a child who is not mobile (usually first nine months) is pathognomonic of abuse. Such an injury occurs during feeding or by a blow. The latter is more likely to cause both contusion of the lip and tearing of the frenulum. When the frenulum is torn during feeding it is as a consequence of parental anger or frustration in response to feeding difficulty. A bottle or spoon is forcd into the mouth damaging the frenulum. In mobile children, particularly toddlers who are unstable on their feet, a torn frenulum can occur accidentally. A child may stumble and fall against an item of furniture such as a coffee table. Frenulum tears heal very quickly and seldom require treatment.

Dental injuries may require the assistance of a dentist. Avulsion of a deciduous tooth requires no action. Avulsion of a permanent tooth is a dental emergency. The tooth should be reinserted as soon as possible, the best results being achieved within an hour.If a delay is likely the tooth should be preserved in milk until reimplantation.

Nasal injuries

A blow to the nose may cause bleeding or a deviated septum (see Figure 10.5). A blood clot may be visible in the nose and when the

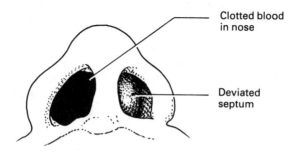

Figure 10.5   Nasal injuries from a blow to the nose.

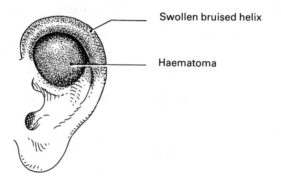

Figure 10.6   'Cauliflower ear' from repeated blows to the ear.

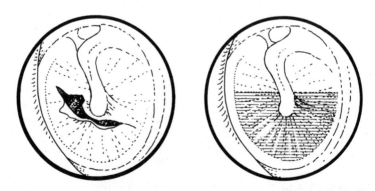

Figure 10.7   A tear of the tympanic membrane (left) and blood behind the ear drum (right). These injuries can be caused by a direct blow or a basal skull fracture.

septum is deviated the nose may be swollen and the septum visible in the nostril.

Ears

It is indeed rare for ear injuries to occur by accident. When children fall they do not injure their ears. Bruised ears are commonly caused by the ears being pulled, pinched or boxed. Repeated blows to the external ear cause bleeding and haematoma formation producing 'cauliflower' ears (see Figure 10.6). A powerful blow directly to the ear can cause rupture of the ear drum or bleeding into the middle ear (see Figure 10.7). A basal skull fracture may also cause bleeding in the middle ear or rupture of the ear drum with leakage of cerebrospinal fluid (see Figure 10.7). Bruising over the mastoid bone (behind the pinna) is associated with basal skull fracture. This is known as Battle's Sign.

Further reading

1. McNeese MC, Hebeler JR. The abused child. A clinical approach to identification and management. *Ciba Clinical Symposia*, volume 29, number 5, 1977.
2. Friendly DS. *Ocular Aspects of Physical Child Abuse in Pediatric Ophthalmology*. Ed. Harley RD. London: WB Saunders, 1983.
3. Levin AV. Ocular manifestations of child abuse. *Ophthalmology Clinics of North America* 1990; **3**: 249–64.
4. Schmitt BD. The child with non-accidental trauma. In: Heffer RE, Kempe RS eds. *The Battered Child*. Chicago: University of Chicago Press, 1987.
5. Lambert WF, Grant P. Recognising and documenting cutaneous signs of child abuse. *Current Opinion in Pediatrics* 1992; **4**: 638–42.
6. Bernat JE. Dental trauma and bite mark evaluation. In: Ludwig S, Kornberg AE eds. *Child Abuse. A Medical Reference*. London: Churchill Livingstone, 1992.
7. Levin AV. Ophthalmologic manifestations. In: Ludwig S, Kornberg AE eds. *Child Abuse. A Medical Reference*. London: Churchill Livingstone, 1992.

11   Thoracic and abdominal injuries

Thoracic injury

Rib fractures are commonly detected in abused children almost all of whom are under two. The vast majority are clinically unsuspected and are usually discovered on the skeletal survey. The ribs of the young child are particularly compliant making them more resilient to fractures from falls and minor trauma. Feldman and Brewer have shown that pressure applied to the chest during cardiac resuscitation does not cause fractures. In the absence of bone disease unexplained rib fractures in the young child are specific for abuse. The exception to this rule is when fractures detected in the first weeks of life are caused by chest compression during the birth process. Rib fractures caused by birth injury are indeed rare. Most fractures occur in the posterior ribs close to the vertebral column (see Figure 11.1). Firm attachment at these points creates the greatest mechanical stress and a predisposition to fracture. Lateral fractures are less common and anterior fractures least common. Rib fractures are usually multiple and may be unilateral or bilateral. Rarely the fracture may puncture the lung causing bleeding (haemothorax) or air (pneumothorax) in the pleural cavity.

The mechanism responsible for most rib fractures is a violent anterior posterior compression of the chest as the infant is grasped and shaken. Rib fractures also occur as a result of blows to the chest, by stamping on the chest or by being thrown against a hard edge. Acute rib fractures may be radiologically invisible and only become apparent ten to 14 days later when callus forms. Scintigraphy is of particular value in detecting rib fractures in the early phase when x-rays are frequently unhelpful.

Fractures of the mid clavicle can occur by accident or as a result of abuse. Fractures of the lateral end together with fractures of the scapula should be considered specific for abuse, particularly in the child under two. They are usually caused by violent traction of the arm, but may result from sudden acceleration/deceleration in the shaken infant (see Shaken Baby Syndrome, Chapter 9).

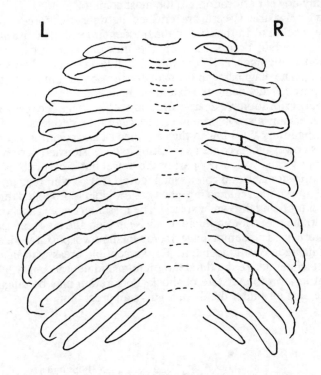

Figure 11.1 Posterior view of thorax showing multiple rib fractures in various stages of healing. Pattern typical of repeated blows or kicks.

Abdominal injury

The incidence of abdominal injury in abused children is less than 2%. Unlike those with inflicted skeletal and head injury most are over two. After head injury abdominal trauma is the most common cause of death, the mortality being about 40–50%. The high mortality is in part attributable to the frequent delay in diagnosis. Very many children have no marks or bruises on the abdomen to indicate the cause of their distress thereby creating diagnostic confusion. Most injuries occur from a forceful blow or kick to the abdomen. Bruising may not occur as the abdominal wall is relaxed and provides little resistance; the brunt of the force being borne by the internal organs.

1. Hollow viscera

Hollow visceral injuries are almost as frequent as injuries of the solid organs. Intramural haematoma of the duodenum and jejunum followed by bowel perforation are the most common.

Fixed epigastric viscera are crushed between the force and the vertebral column. In the case of the duodenum, with its rich vascular supply, bleeding occurs between the mucosal and serosal layers. The upper abdomen is tender and the child may have bile-stained vomiting. The diagnosis can be made by ultrasound, but x-ray studies are required to delineate the extent of the lesion.

Bowel perforation, vessel rupture and haemorrhage occur as a result of two mechanisms: compression and acceleration/deceleration forces (whipping injury). A blow to the abdomen causes compression of the gaseous bowel and its contents resulting in distension and perforation. Such injury can involve any part of the bowel but is particularly common in the stomach and colon (see Figure 11.2). A whipping injury is caused by a sudden change in velocity as the child is propelled through the air after being thrown or struck. The mesentery which anchors the bowel to the posterior abdominal wall is stressed and may tear causing mesenteric vessel haemorrhage and/or small bowel perforation at the site of ligamentous attachment. The susceptible areas with ligamentous attachments are the duodenojejunum and ileocaecum. Children present in a profound state of shock. Perforation may be diagnosed by detecting air under the diaphragm in an erect film.

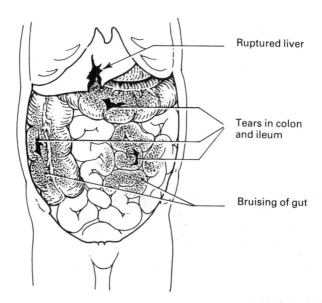

Ruptured liver

Tears in colon and ileum

Bruising of gut

Figure 11.2   Bowel perforation and liver rupture from repeated blows to the abdomen.

2. Solid viscera

The liver is the solid organ most frequently injured by inflicted injury. Unlike accidental injuries the vast majority of inflicted injuries involve the exposed epigastric part on the left side (see Figure 11.3). The clinical presentation of liver injury may vary from no abdominal pain, mild pain to profound shock. Liver enzymes are helpful in detecting occult liver injury. While the spleen and kidney are the most frequently injured organs in blunt accidental injury they are rarely injured by physical abuse. Kidney injury is the more frequent and may be accompanied by massive haematuria. When investigation is deemed necessary the diagnosis of liver, spleen and kidney injury is best made by CT scan.

Although severe pancreatic injury (Figure 11.4) is rare owing to its deep location in the abdomen, traumatic pancreatitis is commonly observed in abdominal trauma from physical abuse. Trauma is the most common cause of childhood pancreatitis. The child will present with peritonitis and damage to other internal organs will need to be excluded. The diagnosis can be confirmed by a raised serum and/or urinary amylase level. The pancreatic inflammation may be localised by adjacent organs forming a fibrous capsule known as a pseudocyst

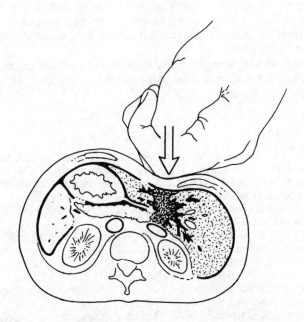

Figure 11.3 Left liver lobe injury from a blow to the epigastrium.

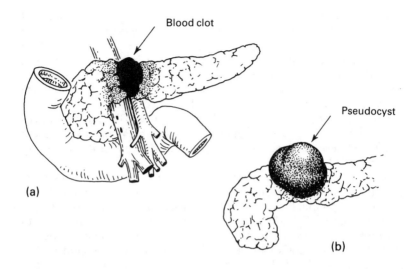

Figure 11.4   (a) Pancreatic transection and (b) the formation of a pancreatic pseudocyst.

(see Figure 11.4). Two to three weeks after injury the patient presents with an upper abdominal mass. Ultrasonography is helpful in identifying pancreatic trauma initially and subsequently demonstrating cyst formation.

Children with abdominal trauma require immediate resuscitation after which the expert advice of a paediatric surgeon should be obtained.

Further reading

1. Hatter JA. Injuries of the gastro-intestinal tract in children. Notes on recognition and management. *Clinical Pediatrics* 1966; **5**: 476–80.
2. Feldman KW, Brewer DK. Child abuse, cardiopulmonary resuscitation and rib fractures. *Pediatrics* 1984; **73**: 339–42.
3. Kleinman PK. *Diagnostic Imaging of Child Abuse*. Baltimore: Williams and Wilkins, 1987.
4. Cooper A et al. Major blunt abdominal trauma due to child abuse. *Journal of Trauma* 1988; **28**: 1483–6.
5. Ledbetter DJ et al. Diagnostic and surgical inplications of child abuse. *Archives of Surgery* 1988; **123**: 1101–5.
6. Carty H. Skeletal manifestations of child abuse. *Bone, Clinical and Biochemical News and Reviews* 1989; **6**: 3–7.
7. Merton DF, Carpenter BLM. Radiologic imaging of inflicted injury in the Child Abuse Syndrome. *Pediatric Clinics of North America* 1990; **37**: 815–37.

8. Coant PN et al. Markers of occult liver injury in cases of physical abuse in children. *Pediatrics* 1992; **89**: 274–8.
9. Cooper A. Thoraco-abdominal trauma. In: Ludwig S, Kornberg AE eds. *Child Abuse. A Medical Reference*. London: Churchill Livingstone, 1992.
10. Barry PW, Hocking MD. Infant rib fracture – birth trauma or non-accidental injury. *Archives of Disease of Childhood* 1993; **68**: 250.

12   Bone trauma

After bruising, fractures are the most common form of limb trauma. As long ago as 1860 Tardieu published an article which clearly identified abuse-related fractures in children who had been killed by means such as whipping and burning. He drew attention to their repeated fractures which were attributed to rickets. In 1946 Caffey described an association between subdural haematomas and long bone fractures; such injuries being reported to be of traumatic origin by Silverman in 1953. Wooley and Evans in 1955 were the first to note that fractures in children were often wilfully inflicted. Seven years later Kempe and his colleagues coined the phrase 'battered child syndrome' in their classic paper in the *Journal of the American Medical Association*.

The long bones most commonly fractured are the humerus, tibia and femur. The difficulty with fractures in young children is that with the exception of metaphyseal-epiphyseal injuries there is nothing specific to child abuse. As always the history and level of development of the child is of paramount importance in deciding whether the x-ray changes were accidental or inflicted. The presence of multiple fractures, particularly of differing age, is very suggestive of abuse. However, about half the non-accidental fractures are single.

Limb injuries are of three types:

1. Diaphyseal fractures

These are the most common, the fracture line being spiral (oblique) or transverse. In a large series involving 429 fractures King found transverse fractures to be the most common.[1]

Direct blows usually cause transverse fractures but may cause spiral fractures. Transverse fractures are also caused by a bending type of force. Spiral fractures are usually caused by a twisting force (see Figure 12.1). A long bone fracture in a child below age three should strongly raise the suspicion of child abuse. This is particularly so in the first year when a child is unable to run so that a fracture of the tibia or femur cannot be attributed to a twisting injury while running and falling. A humeral fracture accompanied by finger mark bruising of the limb or an Erbs palsy (brachial plexus injury – see Figure 12.2) strongly suggests abuse. It should, however, be noted

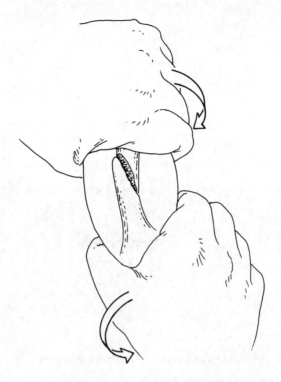

Figure 12.1 The typical twisting movement causing a spiral fracture of the tibia.

that it is common for long bone injuries to be induced without any obvious bruising.

2. Metaphyseal-epiphyseal fractures

In infancy these fractures are pathognomonic of child abuse. They are caused by wrenching and twisting the extremities. Similar injuries can occur when the child is violently shaken and the limbs are allowed to dangle and lash back and forth. Symmetrical bilateral lesions suggest shaking as the cause. Fractures occur through the most immature part of the bone, the metaphyseal primary spongiosa. The periosteum is lightly attached to the metaphysis and is seldom disrupted. These fractures heal from the growth plate. Absence of callus formation makes them particularly difficult to date. Metaphyseal fractures appear to cause surprisingly little pain, tenderness and swelling. The absence of clinical signs and callus formation may create diagnostic uncertainty in the unwary.

Figure 12.2   An Erb's palsy caused by trauma of the upper arm.

Birth injury, particularly breach delivery can cause metaphyseal injury. Metaphyseal fractures also occur in osteogenesis imperfection but should not cause diagnostic confusion as there will be other bony abnormalities.

The young child who falls on an outstretched arm is more likely to sustain a metaphyseal cortical fracture. As the child gets older the cortex strengthens and such a fall is likely to damage the relatively weaker part of the bone causing metaphyseal-epiphyseal injury.

There are two classical x-ray patterns of metaphyseal-epiphyseal injuries. The first is a radiolucent line across the metaphysis with an avulsed chip of metaphysis (see Figures 12.3 and 12.4). This pattern is variously known as the 'chip', 'corner' or Salter II fracture. The other is the 'bucket handle' fracture when a crescentic piece of metaphysis is widely separated (see Figure 12.4). It is now known that both patterns result from the same pathologic injury and are simply variations in radiographic appearance due to different projections. The basic lesion is a planar fracture through the primary spongiosa of the metaphysis with a disk-like fragment of bone and calcified cartilage. The radiographic appearance of a 'chip' of metaphysis is an illusion created by a tangential view. When the projection is oblique

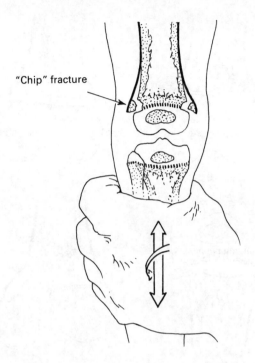

"Chip" fracture

Figure 12.3 Typical 'chip' fractures of the femur and the mechanism of injury.

the dense peripheral margin of the disk-like fragment appears crescentic ('bucket handle').

Injuries which are rarely found are Salter I and Salter III fractures (see Figure 12.4). The Salter-Harris classification is widely used and is primarily based on the x-ray appearance of the fracture. A Salter I fracture is one in which metaphyseal separation occurs without or with minimal displacement because the periosteum remains intact. Fractures of the physeal plate (Salter III) are caused by violent traction and rotation and are commonly complicated by growth disturbance.

3. Periosteal new bone formation ('bone bruising')

This reflects traumatic separation of the diaphyseal periosteum which occurs when the bone is tightly gripped, squeezed, pulled or twisted. Subperiosteal haemorrhage occurs and is followed by new bone formation one to two weeks later (see Figure 12.5). When symmetrical it may be confused with physiological periostitis, a normal find-

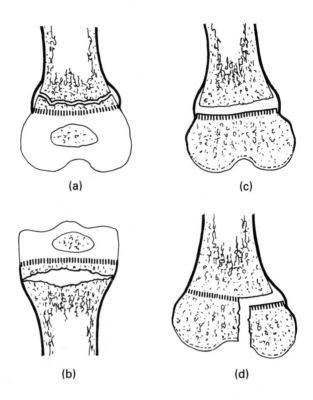

(a)

(c)

(b)

(d)

Figure 12.4 Metaphyseal fractures: (a) – Salter-Harris Type II ('chip' fracture); (b) – Bucket handle fracture; (c) – Salter-Harris Type I; (d) – Salter-Harris Type III.

ing between two and eight months. Unlike 'bone bruising', which may extend to the lower metaphysis, physiologic periostitis is always confined to the diaphysis. If there is any doubt scintigraphy will distinguish the two. Periostitis may also be caused by infection (e.g. congenital syphilis) and a variety of metabolic disorders such as rickets, copper deficiency, vitamin A intoxication and scurvy.

Hand and foot fractures

Fractures of fingers, toes and small bones of hands and feet are occasionally found. 'Knuckle beating' fractures caused by punishment are generally random in distribution. Contiguous fractures of phalanges and metacarpals/tarsals are often due to a stamping or trampling injury.

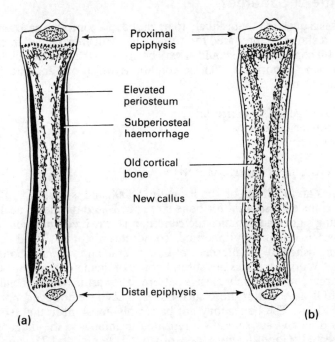

Proximal
epiphysis

Elevated
periosteum

Subperiosteal
haemorrhage

Old cortical
bone

New callus

Distal epiphysis

(a)

(b)

Figure 12.5 Sequence of bone changes following bone trauma (a) acute trauma, (b) healing phase.

How old is the fracture?

This is a question frequently asked of the expert. It needs to be emphasised that dating a fracture is an imprecise science and banding is merely a rough guide. As a general rule the younger the child the faster a fracture heals.

Early periosteal reaction is visible four to ten days after injury with a peak incidence of first appearance at about seven days. Soft callus (hazy calcification) is evident at two to three weeks and hard callus (dense calcification) at three to six weeks. Remodelling of the bone occurs at about a year but varies considerably depending on age, initial deformity and amount of callus.

In most fractures a line can be discerned; however some hairline fractures are not radiologically evident. Generally a fracture line in the shaft of a long bone remains visible from four to eight weeks. Refracture through an old untreated fracture can be recognised by a well-defined fracture line in an area of dense callus.

Brittle or battered?

This is a question that is likely to be raised in a contested case and the expert should be prepared for it. In a child with unexplained fractures careful consideration should always be given to the remote possibility of a bone abnormality. Three conditions which can and should be excluded are:

1. osteogenesis imperfecta,
2. copper deficiency,
3. rickets.

1. Osteogenesis imperfecta (OI)

OI has an incidence of about one in 20 000 and is caused by defective collagen, essential for bone strength. Based on the clinical presenting signs and genetics the condition is classified into four types. Type I is dominantly inherited, constitutes about 80% and can be distinguished by the presence of blue sclerae and wormian bones on x-ray. Wormian bones are sutural bones of diameter 6 mm by 4 mm or larger, arranged in a mosaic pattern. The vast majority of children with OI have ten or more such bones. They are, however, not specific to OI. The bones may not be readily apparent in the neonatal period and x-rays should be repeated in infancy if the diagnosis is suspected. Good quality x-rays of frontal, lateral and Towne views may be needed. It should also be noted that many normal infants have a blue tinge to the sclerae in the first three to four months.

Type II (blue sclerae) and the milder Type III are genetically heterogeneous, new mutations being autosomal dominant and recessive inheritance being rare. These types have multiple fractures and skeletal deformity. Type II die *in utero* or in the perinatal period, while Type III have wormian bones and other features of OI (see Table 12.1). The bony changes are more severe than Types I and IV making the diagnosis readily apparent. The greatest difficulty in distinguishing OI from abuse arises in the case of Type IV (white sclerae). This is particularly so in those very rare instances when a child has fractures, a normal skeleton (no wormian bones) and no family history. In such a situation the distinction between abuse and OI becomes very difficult. The expert witness should, however, make the court aware that the probability of OI in such a scenario is more than one in a million. In a large city of 6000 births annually such a case of OI is likely to arise every 100–300 years. The salient features of OI are shown in the table. It is imperative that when a child presents with unexplained fractures a detailed family history should be taken and features of OI sought. The sclerae, teeth and hearing of parents should be checked.

Table 12.1 Summary of the main features of osteogenesis imperfecta

1. Bone fragility, fractures,* osteoporosis
2. Blue sclerae (Type I and Type II)
3. Wormian bones
4. Defective dentition
5. Hearing impairment
6. Ligament laxity and hypermobility of joints
7. Easy bruising
8. Growth retardation
9. Spinal deformity

In the case of a new mutation family members will have none of these features.

*Unlike abuse, fractures occur even while in a protective environment.

2. Copper deficiency.

Copper is an indispensable trace element, deficiency causing abnormal bone collagen. Bone changes include fractures (never skull), osteoporosis, periostitis, metaphyseal cupping and spur formation. It can be differentiated from non-accidental injury by having symmetrical skeletal changes and by a low serum copper and caeruloplasmin level. Blood changes (neutropaenia and anaemia) are usual.

Copper deficiency is rare and is confined to premature infants, particularly those who have been parenterally fed. There has never been a report of copper deficiency in a healthy term infant fed breast milk or an infant formula marketed in Britain.

3. Rickets

Very low birth weight infants (< 1.5 kg) sometimes develop rickets and have fractures. These infants are easily distinguished by their abnormal bone texture and other bone changes such as periostitis and metaphyseal cupping. The blood alkaline phosphatase level is usually elevated.

Birth trauma

It should always be borne in mind that fractures detected in the neonatal period might have been sustained at birth. Birth injuries such as a fractured clavicle are common and often pass unnoticed. The incidence of cephalohaematomas in the newborn is 1–2% of which about 5% are associated with an underlying linear skull fracture. Confusion with abuse might arise when the cephalohaematoma persists for a month or two, particularly when associated with a fracture.

Rarely depressed skull fractures occur *in utero*. These are thought to be caused by compression of the skull by a bony prominence such as the sacral promontory or symphysis pubis. Other infrequent birth injuries are those involving the ribs and long bones, mainly the humerus and femur. Such injuries occur mainly in large babies when delivery is difficult.

Radiologic investigations

The need for investigation should be considered on an individual basis. Factors which will determine the need for investigation are age, history, type of injury and the likelihood of litigation. The x-rays of children with head injuries are frequently supplemented with a CT scan/MRI or both. Radiologic investigation of head injuries is discussed in Chapter 8, Head injuries, and Chapter 9, Shaken Baby Syndrome.

The skeletal survey

The purpose of the skeletal survey is to highlight occult fractures. When fractures are found, varying age would indicate that the child was repeatedly abused. In the presence of fractures normal bone architecture would help eliminate an underlying bone disease. The unexpected finding of fractures in a child with a minor injury throws a new complexion on the case affording the child better protection. A skeletal survey is mandatory in all children with suspected physical abuse below age two. It is of little value beyond five. Between two and five each case should be considered on an individual basis bearing in mind that an occult fracture is less likely the older and more articulate the child.

The following radiographs are required:

1. Skull, AP* and lateral.
2. Chest, spine and pelvis, AP (on one film). In infancy lateral views of the axial skeleton are obtained because of the occurrence of fractures involving the spine and sternum.
3. AP views of the long bones including the hands.

Any suspicious areas should be supplemented with local views. Oblique views of the ribs and both AP and lateral views of joints

---

*AP = Anterior Posterior.

will often clarify suspicious lesions. Rib and metaphyseal fractures may only be visible in one view. A radiologist should monitor the technical quality of the films, which should be labelled with the name, date and side. If the time is not recorded on the film it should be recorded on the request card. In the case of equivocal lesions, particularly rib fractures, it may be necessary to repeat the survey in one to two weeks. On occasion it may be necessary to repeat the survey when the first was normal if bony injury is strongly suspected. A second survey may also help date fractures.

Isotope bone scanning (scintigraphy) which provides less radiation than conventional x-rays is sometimes used as a supplement to the skeletal survey. It is more sensitive for rib fractures, subtle, undisplaced shaft fractures and early areas of periosteal reaction. Metaphyseal-epiphyseal fractures, especially when bilateral, some vertebral and many skull fractures are undetectable by this technique. The Radiology Committee of the American Academy of Pediatrics (see Haller *et al*) recommends against bone scanning as a primary tool.[2] Many district general hospitals in Britain do not have isotope facilities.

References

1. King J, Diefendorf D, Apthorp J, Nigrete VF, Carlson M. Analysis of 429 fractures in 189 battered children. *Journal of Pediatric Orthopedics* 1988; **8**: 585–9.
2. Haller JO et al. Diagnostic imaging of child abuse. *Pediatrics* 1991; **87**: 262–4.
3. Garza Mercado R. Intrauterine depressed skull fractures of the newborn. *Neurosurgery* 1982; **10**: 694–7.
4. Ellerstein NS, Norris KJ. Value of radiologic skeletal survey in assessment of abused children. *Pediatrics* 1984; **59**: 860–4.
5. Warlock P, Stower M, Barbor P. Patterns of fractures in accidental and non-accidental injury in children: a comparative study. *British Medical Journal* 1986; **293**: 100–2.
6. Kleinman PK. *Diagnostic Imaging of Child Abuse*. Baltimore: Williams and Wilkins, 1987.
7. Chapman S. Child abuse or copper deficiency? A radiological view. *British Medical Journal* 1987; **294**: 1370.
8. Taitz LS. Child abuse and osteogenesis imperfecta. *British Medical Journal* 1987; **295**: 1082–3.
9. Joffe M, Ludwig S. Stairway injuries in children. *Pediatrics* 1988; **82**: 457–61.
10. Carty H. Brittle or battered. *Archives of Disease in Childhood* 1988; **63**: 350–2.
11. Ablin DS, Greenspan A, Reinhart M, Grix A. Differentiation of child abuse from osteogenesis imperfecta. *American Journal of Radiology* 1990; **154**: 1035–46.
12. Dalton HJ, Slovis T, Helfer RE, Comstock J, Schewer S, Riolo S.

Undiagnosed abuse in children younger than 3 years with femoral fracture. *American Journal of Diseases in Children* 1990; **144**: 875–8.

13. Merten DF, Carpenter BLM. Radiologic imaging of inflicted injury in the child abuse syndrome. *Pediatric Clinics of North America* 1990; **37**: 815–37.

14. Thomas S, Rosenfield NS, Leventhal JM, Marcovitz RI. Long bone fractures in young children: distinguishing accidental injuries from child abuse. *Pediatrics* 1991; **88**: 471–6.

15. Loder RT, Bookout C. Fracture patterns in battered children. *Journal of Orthopaedic Trauma* 1991; **5**: 428–33.

16. Swischuk LE. Radiographic signs of skeletal trauma. In: Ludwig S, Kornberg AE eds. *Child Abuse. A Medical Reference*. London: Churchill Livingstone, 1992.

17. Chapman S. The radiological dating of injuries. *Archives of Disease in Childhood* 1992; **67**: 1063–5.

18. Chapman S. Recent advances in the radiology of child abuse. In: Hobbs CJ, Wynne JM eds. *Child Abuse*. London: Baillière Tindall, 1993.

13   Burns and scalds

Thermal injury is common in children between nine months and five years. Approximately 10% of injuries are inflicted, the rest occur accidentally on many occasions as a result of parental carelessness or neglect. Very rarely disturbed children may burn themselves. It is frequently difficult to distinguish an accidental burn from an inflicted one. Both inflicted and accidental burns can occur at similar sites, however burns on the buttocks, perineum and back of hand are more commonly inflicted. Factors which help in making the distinction are:

1. The age of the child. Children who are able to get about and reach out are very likely to be accidentally injured.
2. The physical characteristics of the burn. This may help identify the implement used.
3. The history. A vague, inconsistent or implausible history particularly with failure or delay in seeking medical attention, should raise strong suspicion about non-accidental injury.

Most non-accidental injuries are dry burns or scalds. Occasionally friction burns are seen as a result of a child being dragged on a carpet or as a result of a ligature being tied around the wrists, ankles or neck. Burns caused by dragging involve bony prominences. Chemical, electrical and microwave burns are exceedingly rare abusive injuries in Britain.

Dry burns frequently occur as a consequence of misguided chastisement meted out to the child. The child who plays with a cigarette lighter may be burned with the lighter to 'teach him a lesson'. In such cases the metal edge of the lighter and wheels are heated leaving a characteristic brand mark. The vast majority of dry burns are caused by cigarettes, lighters, radiators, heaters and household items such as irons (see Figure 13.1) and stoves. The child is punished by being held against the heater or radiator or the heat source (for example an iron) is held against the child's skin. The bars of a heater leave a 'grid' pattern and the iron shape (see Figure 13.1) make identification easy. While it is possible to brush against a lighted cigarette and sustain a burn, such a burn would differ from an inflicted burn in that it would not be well delineated and circular. Inflicted cigarette burns have a pattern reflecting deliberation on the part of the

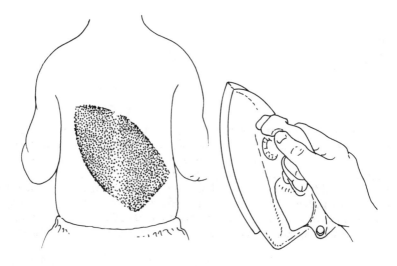

Figure 13.1 Imprint of iron on back of child. It would be impossible for such a burn to occur accidentally.

abuser. They are generally sharply circumscribed, the diameter measuring 5–8 mm (see Figure 13.2). The edge may be indurated and the centre blistered or escharotic. Cigarette burns need to be distinguished from impetigo and ecthyma which may mimic cigarette burns in that they may also have a circular appearance with a central scabbed area. These lesions are often accompanied by skin infection elsewhere and the degree of inflammation is more pronounced. Unlike cigarette burns there is a wide variation in the width of lesions. Other skin conditions which may cause diagnostic confusion are discrete lesions of psoriasis or eczema. Cigarette burns are frequently inflicted on exposed parts such as the hands and arms. Burns on parts of the body normally covered are unlikely to be accidental as clothing provides protection.

Scalds are caused by dunking the child in hot water or by running hot water on the child. Such actions are used as a form of punishment often related to difficulties with bowel or bladder control. A small percentage of children are scalded by having hot liquids thrown at them. Such incidents occur on impulse in a fit of rage.

Dunking scalds involve dipping the buttocks, arms or legs in hot water (see Figure 13.3). When limbs are exposed the water level produces a characteristic 'glove or stocking' circumferential appearance. The sharp margin together with absence of splash marks implies restraint. A child free to move would try to extricate himself by thrashing about so causing splashes and blurring of the water line.

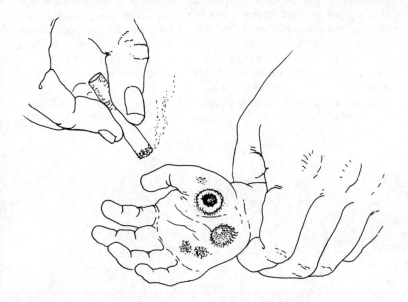

Figure 13.2 Cigarette burns in various stages of healing. Cigarette burns are usually inflicted on palms, arms, soles and buttocks.

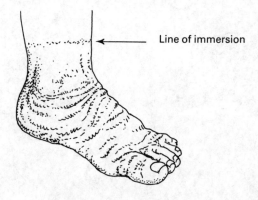

Line of immersion

Figure 13.3 Typical dunking scald in which the foot was immersed in hot water.

When the thighs are held against the abdomen as the buttocks and perineum are dunked in hot water the opposed areas of the abdomen and thighs will be spared (see Figure 13.4). Should the buttocks be pressed against the base of the container the cooler base will cause areas of contact to be spared. In dunking scalds the position of the water line and the areas of skin sparing enable the position of immersion to be reconstructed (Figure 13.4).

Scalds caused by deliberate exposure to running tap water or thrown hot liquids are particularly difficult to distinguish from accidental

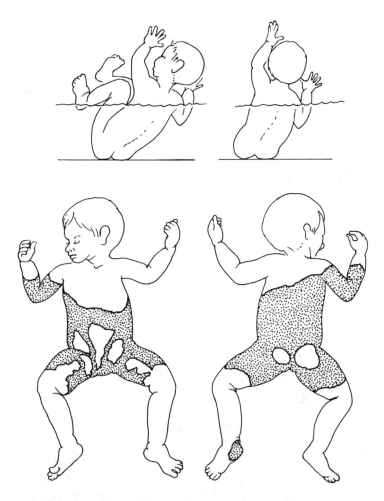

Figure 13.4   Position of immersion and areas of skin sparing.

scalds. Deliberate tap water scalds are often on the buttocks or back of hands which should arouse suspicion. Burns from thrown liquids frequently have an excessive number of splash burns around the primary site and the distribution might be different from that resulting from an accident. For example a child reaching up to pull over a hot kettle could be expected to be burnt below the chin, on the axilla and anterior chest. Scalds not involving these sites should arouse suspicion when such an explanation is proffered. It may be possible to determine the direction of the hot water by observing the depth of the burn and the pattern of water flow. The area of initial contact will be the most deeply burned; the water then cooling with less scalding as it runs downwards by gravity.

In medico-legal work doctors are often asked to provide information about the cause, timing, severity and healing of burns. Cognisance should be given to the fact that a small number of children are burned by siblings and that in some cultures children may be burned as part of folk medicine. Phytophotodermatitis (skin exposure to a phototoxic plant or its juices and sunshine) may simulate scalds or bruises. Severe ammoniacal (napkin) dermatitis or a fixed drug eruption may be confused with a burn by the unwary. When giving an opinion about the cause of a burn the following should be considered:

1. The temperature of the source.
2. The type of clothing worn, if any.
3. The duration of exposure bearing in mind the natural tendency to withdraw immediately from a source of discomfort.

In determining the temperature of the source it may be necessary to visit the home, examine an appliance or consult with a heating engineer. Figure 13.5 shows the water temperature required to induce a full thickness scald against time. The figure is based on adult skin; the time required for a full thickness burn in the thinner skin of a child would be considerably shorter. In the USA the safety aspect of household water temperature has been taken on board by paediatricians and in some states it is limited to below 54°C by law. In Britain there are no restrictions on domestic water temperature.

It is extremely difficult to 'time' a burn with any accuracy. Although the extent of healing may assist, the wide variation makes any estimate imprecise. The rate of healing will depend on the severity and factors such as the presence or absence of infection.

The severity of a burn depends not only on the extent of involvement of surface area but also the depth. The three layers of the skin are the superficial epidermis, the dermis and the deep layer containing subdermal fat. The epidermis is a keratinised epithelium in which new cells are constantly being produced by mitosis in the basal layer.

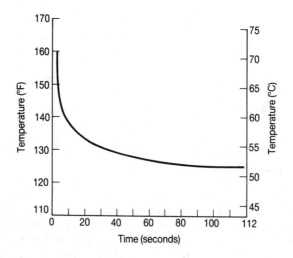

Figure 13.5   Time temperature relationship required to induce a full thickness scald of adult skin. (Graph adapted from Moritz and Henriques.)[1]

The dermis contains blood vessels, nerves and hair follicles, sweat and sebaceous glands. A burn wound may extend through the entire thickness of the skin, or it may damage or destroy only part of the skin. Clinically, the depth of the burn is determined by its colour and the presence or absence of sensation, blister formation or loss of elasticity. A simple classification of burns based on depth is:

1. superficial burns,
2. partial thickness burns,
3. full thickness burns.

1. Superficial burns

A superficial burn is characterised by mild pain and erythema that blanches when pressure is applied but rapidly recurs when pressure is removed. This type involves only the surface epithelium (keratin layer). A superficial burn will heal within two to three days and healing may be accompanied by flaking or peeling of the injured epithelium. A typical sunburn is an example of such a burn.

2. Partial thickness burns

Partial thickness burns involve the deeper layers of epithelium, i.e. those beneath the surface (keratin layer), and may be either superficial or deep. Superficial partial thickness burns are characterised by erythema, blister formation, oedema and pain. This type may heal spontaneously within seven to ten days with only mild scarring. Deep partial thickness burns result in the destruction not only of the epidermis but the upper levels of dermis as well (see Figure 13.6(a)). Skin appendages such as hair follicles, sweat glands and sebaceous glands remain intact. If infection does not occur, these may heal without grafting, with epithelium from the skin appendages spreading to cover the surface of the burn in three to four weeks. Scarring may be severe. Initially, a deep partial thickness burn may be marble-white and oedematous. If superficial nerve endings are destroyed, the patient will experience little pain.

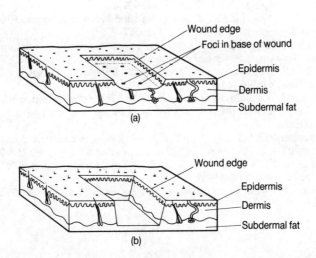

Figure 13.6 (a) A partial thickness wound of skin. Re-epithelialisation occurs from the edge of the wound and from the epithelial foci provided by hair shafts and sweat ducts within the base of the wound. (b) A full thickness wound of skin. Re-epithelialisation can only occur from the edge of the wound. During the course of healing a new tissue, granulation tissue, forms to fill the wound cavity. Over a long period this eventually becomes fibrous. The epithelium covering the healed wound is relatively fragile and can be readily damaged making skin grafting necessary.

3. Full thickness burns

Full thickness burns involve the destruction of all the skin and its appendages (see Figure 13.6(b)). These may vary in appearance from marble-white to mahogany-coloured with thrombosed veins to charred, dry burns. There is little if any oedema and such burns are usually not painful to touch. Full thickness burns of significant size do not heal spontaneously and grafting is required.

References

1. Moritz AR, Henriques FC. Studies of thermal injury: the relative importance of time and temperature in the causation of cutaneous burns. *American Journal of Pathology* 1947; **23**: 695–720.
2. Keen JH, Lendrum J, Wolman B. Inflicted burns and scalds in children. *British Medical Journal* 1975; **1**: 268–9.
3. Lenoski EF, Hunter K. Specific pattern of inflicted burn injuries. *Journal of Trauma* 1977; **17**: 842–6.
4. Feldman KW, Scholler RT, Feldman JA, McMillan M. Tap–water scald burns in children. *Pediatrics* 1978; **62**: 1–7.
5. Sandler AP, Haynes V. Non-accidental trauma and medical folk belief: a case of cupping. *Pediatrics* 1978; **61**: 921–2.
6. Hight DW, Bokalar HR, Lloyd J. Inflicted burns in children. Recognition and treatment. *JAMA* 1979; **242**: 517–20.
7. Caffman K, Boyce T, Hansen C. Phytophotodermatitis simulating child abuse. *Journal of American Diseases in Childhood* 1985; **139**: 239–40.
8. Hobbs CJ. When are burns accidental? *Archives of Disease in Childhood* 1986; **61**: 357–61.
9. Feldman KW. Child abuse by burning. In: Helfer RE, Kempe RS, eds. *The Battered Child* (4th edn.). Chicago: Chicago University Press, 1987: 197–213.
10. Alexander RC, Surre JA, Cohle SD. Microwave oven burns to children: an unusual manifestation of child abuse. *Pediatrics* 1987; **79**: 255–260.
11. Donnaker CJ, Glover RA, Goltz RW. Phytophotodermatitis. *Clinical Pediatrics* 1988; **27**: 289–90.
12. Prescott PR. Hair dryer burns in children. *Pediatrics* 1990; **86**: 692–7.

14 Sexual abuse

The true incidence of child sexual abuse is not known. Frequent media reports of children who have been sexually abused attest to its high prevalence across the social spectrum. Allegations of sexual abuse are common during parental separation or divorce, particularly when custody arrangements are disputed. Such allegations are frequently unsubstantiated.

There is accumulating evidence that some children who have been sexually abused are likely to develop adult mental health problems. While most sexually abused children do not have physical signs it is incumbent upon the medical profession to detect such signs when present. In view of the highly emotive nature of such a diagnosis and its attendant social and legal ramifications, extreme diligence is required. Because of the frequent lack of physical signs, the diagnosis is often arrived at in 'jigsaw' fashion based on corroborative evidence of the child and others. Unlike care proceedings, where the verdict is based on a balance of probability, criminal courts require proof beyond reasonable doubt. In a recent review (De Jong and Rose) of convictions for sexual abuse it was concluded that the quality of the history and the verbal ability of the child to tell his/her story are more important than physical signs in securing a conviction.[1]

It cannot be emphasised too strongly that the most valid corroborative evidence can best be obtained by the closest co-operation between doctor, social worker, police and other professionals concerned with the welfare of the child. To avoid distressing the child unnecessarily, interviews should ideally be undertaken jointly by specialist social workers and police officers and need to be videotaped. The setting for such disclosure interviews must be friendly and informal. Toys, anatomically correct dolls and drawing utensils should be readily available. See page 20 for information on the conduct of the interview.

The examination

It is essential that doctors carrying out examinations for sexual abuse be fully acquainted with the normal anatomy of children and correct terminology of female genitalia (Figure 14.1). Anatomic details should be recorded on 'genital charts' (Figures 14.1 and 14.2) and physical details involving other parts of the body on body charts. In

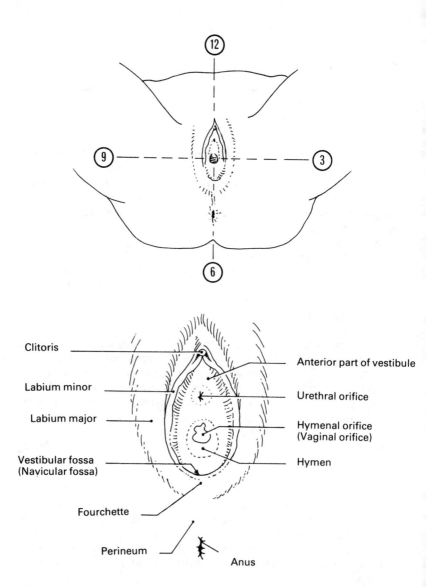

Figure 14.1 Female genital chart. Schematic representation of the perineum of a prepubertal girl with the child lying on her back in the supine frog-leg position. The labia majora are retracted to allow visualisation of the hymen. The numbers (3, 6, 9, 12) have been superimposed to show the orientation of the perineal structures with the face of a clock.

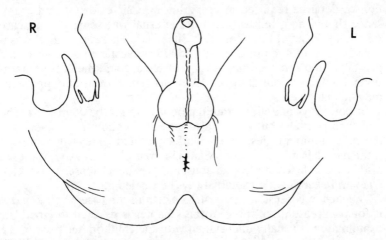

Figure 14.2 Male genital chart.

Britain this work is mainly undertaken by police surgeons (general practitioners) and paediatricians. Access to a forensic science laboratory can only be obtained through the police. The Home Office recommends that doctors undertaking such work should have further training. Courses arranged by the police have been held at various centres. Further to the Cleveland Inquiry, in some parts of the United Kingdom examinations are done jointly by police surgeon and paediatrician, the former being responsible for the forensic and the latter the civil aspects of the case. Having two contemporaneous opinions is cited as a means of avoiding further examinations. The disadvantage is that it is often inconvenient to organise and expensive. Furthermore, there is no evidence that accuracy is improved. A more equitable arrangement would be for one of the doctors to be instructed by the alleged perpetrator or his solicitors from a local panel of suitably trained doctors, an arrangement similar to that for forensic autopsies. In the USA, unlike Britain, a colposcope is widely used for sexual abuse examinations. The good light source, magnification and excellent photographic potential render repeat examinations unnecessary. An independent expert opines on the photographic material. In Britain a single examiner can avoid repeat examinations for second opinions by assiduously documenting the physical signs by both drawing and photography. The expert services of a professional medical photographer will usually be required.

The examination should be done in a relaxed, unhurried, friendly manner in surroundings where the child is made to feel at ease. Where possible the child should be made aware of the procedure in age-appropriate language, and repeated reassurance that the reason for the examination is not his/her fault should be given. Meticulous attention to detail is required in preparing forensic evidence and cognisance should be given to the rather unusual way some parents care for the genitalia of their children. Such 'care' includes painful washing of the child's genitalia, frequent and ritualistic inspections of the genitalia, and repeated application of creams and medical preparations. Medical consultation for factitious genital or urinary problems may be made.

In both boys and girls examination should not be confined to the anus and genitalia but should also include the mouth. Valuable evidence of mouth injuries, venereal infections and semen will be missed if the mouth is not examined. Many children who are sexually abused also have evidence of physical abuse; where sexual abuse is suspected a general examination should always be carried out.

Diagnostic confusion more often arises in the case of girls and it is for that reason that more of this Chapter is devoted to girls. The examination is usually undertaken with the child on her back in the 'frog-leg' position, or in the knee-chest position with 'swayed back' posture (Figure 14.3). In the supine position the labia are gently parted and downward lateral traction is applied. Very young children may be more comfortable lying on the mother's lap (Figure 14.4). In the prone position the labia are parted and the perineum is lifted. It is prudent to note the examination position in the casenotes as hymenal configuration is affected by position. Some girls need to be examined in both positions to obtain optimal visualisation of the hymen. The swayed back position is undignified and may upset children or

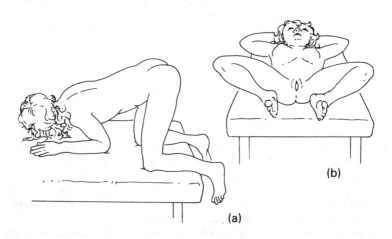

Figure 14.3 The two common examination positions. (a) The prone knee-chest position. (b) The supine 'frog-leg' position. (From Herman-Giddens and Frothingham, 1987.)[6]

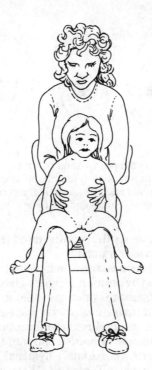

Figure 14.4 Young and frightened children can be examined while sitting on the parent's lap or being held in their arms.

their adult attendants. It should be regarded as the position of second choice.

Physical signs

Girls: There are five common hymenal shapes (Figure 14.5), the crescent and circumferential being most common in the older child. The hymenal edge may be smooth or serrated and bumps or notches do not necessarily indicate abuse. The site of notches is important. Notches do not normally occur between 4 and 8 o'clock. The configuration of the hymen changes throughout childhood, possibly in response to oestrogen. In infancy most are fimbriated whereas the crescentic pattern is predominant in prepubertal girls. With age there is thinning and increased elasticity of the hymen so that at puberty most have a flower-like fimbriated appearance. The elasticity may allow the orifice to be stretched without any physical evidence of trauma and may remain deceptively small. Traumatic appearances of the hymen will vary throughout childhood in line with normal changes

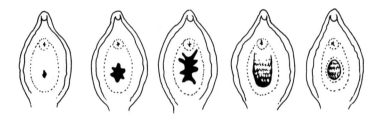

Figure 14.5   The most common hymenal patterns. Annular and denticular are commonly called 'fimbriated'. Variants do occur but are rare. They include septate, imperforate and cribriform hymens and those with openings off centre. (From Herman-Giddens and Frothingham, 1987.)[6]

in configuration. At puberty the oestrogenised redundant hymen may show few signs of previous trauma.

Much attention has been focused on hymenal diameter. As already mentioned it is affected by position, degree of labial traction and, most importantly, by the extent to which the child is relaxed. It increases with age, the mean transverse diameter increasing from <1 mm in infancy to 7 mm at ten years. From the forensic perspective it is the maximal hymenal diameter of normal children that is most relevant. The maximal transverse (horizontal) hymenal diameter of normal children under ten is shown in Table 14.1. When assessing the hymenal diameter the method of measurement should be considered. It is very difficult to measure the hymen accurately and there is bound to be some inaccuracy, particularly when the hymen is contracting and relaxing throughout the examination as often happens. The diverse patterns also raise the question of where measurements should be

Table 14.1   The maximal horizontal diameter of the hymen in normal (non-abuse) children.*

Age (years)	Hymenal diameter (mm)	
	Supine 'frog-leg' position	Knee-chest position
< 2	2	3†
2–5	8	7.5
5–8	9	8.5
8–10	10.5	11

* Vertical diameter may be up to 5 mm more.
† Supine knee-chest position.
(Data from Goff et al (1989) and McCann et al (1990)b.

made. In Britain many police surgeons use Glaister-Keen rods for defining the hymen and facilitating close examination. Measurement with a colposcope is easier but its use is not essential as it does not improve the accuracy of diagnosis.

There are a number of reports which indicate that an intact hymen of normal diameter does not preclude penile or digital penetration. When the hymen is injured by attempted penile penetration the injuries usually occur in the posterior part, between 3 and 9 o'clock, and in the posterior fourchette. Unlike attempted intercourse, where the angle of thrust is different, digital and object injuries usually occur on the anterior part of the hymen, but can occur anywhere. In my experience force is not often used in sexual abuse and the injuries seldom suggest violence.

Diagnostic changes are laceration or scars in the hymen which may extend to the posterior vaginal wall, or loss of hymenal tissue due to previous injury. A midline, white avascular streak of the posterior vestibule may give the impression of a scar, but such a structure is normal in infancy. Labial adhesions which are commonly found in girls between two months and seven years have also been reported in association with posterior fourchette injuries.

The skin around the genitalia should be examined for evidence of rubbing, bruising and inflammation. Vulvovaginitis caused by irritants, threadworms, haemophilus and streptococcal infections is common in girls and causes bleeding and genito-urinary symptoms which may arouse suspicion of sex abuse. Skin diseases rarely cause diagnostic confusion. Those that do cause confusion are lichen sclerosus, flexural psoriasis and Crohn's disease involving the perineal skin. When in doubt an expert dermatological opinion should be sought.

Straddle injuries are not uncommon and can easily be differentiated from abusive injuries by a careful history and examination. These cause crushing of soft tissue over a solid structure such as the symphysis pubis, ischiopubic ramus, and adductor longus tendon. Compared with injuries due to sexual abuse straddle injuries are more often anterior and unilateral and cause damage to the external rather than internal genital structures. Urethral conditions such as prolapse, caruncle or haemangioma may cause bleeding or anatomical changes which may be confused with sex abuse. The common belief that athletic activities such as gymnastics or horseriding can cause damage to the posterior fourchette and hymen is a myth.

Boys: Like girls most sexually abused boys have no physical evidence of abuse. When physical signs are present there may be bruises on the penis but these are uncommon. Anal and rectal involvement is most common. The anus should be examined with the boy in the left lateral position and should be checked for dilatation, venous engorgement, haematomas, fissures, scars and lacerations. The latter may extend beyond the rectal mucosa onto the perianal skin. Rare signs are funnelling (deep displacement of the anus) and swelling of the perianal margin, giving a 'tyre' effect. The skin around the anus should be inspected for scarring and warts. Anal changes have been well documented photographically by Hobbs and Wynne.[2] Reflex anal dilatation, i.e. anal dilatation lasting at least 2–3 seconds after the buttocks are separated for a period of 30 seconds, was the subject of much media attention during the Cleveland Inquiry. During the dilatation the lower end of the anal canal and rectum can be seen. This must be distinguished from the normal opening and closing (winking anus) which is a natural phenomenon. The presence of reflex anal dilatation should raise the suspicion of abuse, but is not a diagnostic sign. Anal fissures and skin tags can occur normally, as does anal dilatation when there is stool in the rectal ampulla. Dilatation commonly occurs during general anaesthesia and in very ill children. It may be found in children with Crohn's disease, muscular and neurologic problems and is frequently detected postmortem. In the absence of stool in the ampulla dilatation greater than 20 mm is highly suggestive of abuse.

Investigations

Forensic

An outline of the procedure to be followed when abuse is suspected is shown in Figure 14.6. Other than physical signs and microbiological investigation, evidence of abuse can be obtained by detection of pubic hair, semen, saliva and foreign substances. In cases of recent assault the child should be undressed on a clean paper spread sheet to collect any loose particles caught up in the clothing. Moist swabs, which are then frozen, can be used for identifying dry semen and sputum on the perineal skin and other parts of the anatomy. Semen might not only confirm that abuse has taken place but can be used to identify the perpetrator by DNA 'fingerprinting'. Such identification is not possible with saliva. It is also essential that (control) blood samples in ethylenediaminetetracetic acid (frozen and unfrozen) accompany the swabs from the child. A Wood's Lamp, an ultraviolet light, is useful in detecting dried semen on the skin. Dried semen fluoresces a white or yellow/green colour. This test is most useful in the first 28 hours. A positive test can be caused by substances other than semen such as urine. A negative test does not exclude semen.

As most abuse disclosures are made some time after the event it is important that the examiner knows the time scale of semen survival in the various orifices. These are shown in Table 14.2. Seminal analysis involves not only looking for sperm but testing for acid phosphatase, an enzyme secreted by the prostatic gland. A more sensitive test undertaken in some laboratories is the prostate-specific protein

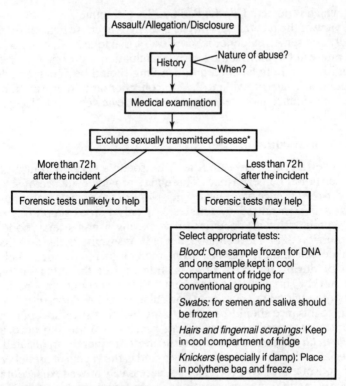

Figure 14.6 A flow chart of the recommended procedure in the management of sexual abuse/assault.

Table 14.2 The time limits for the detection of spermatozoa and seminal fluid. Detection, particularly from the vagina, is highest in the first 24 hours. After 72 hours vaginal detection is rare

	Spermatazoa	*Seminal fluid*
vagina	6 days	12–18 hours
anus	3 days	3 hours
mouth	12–14 hours	–
clothing/bedding	until washed	until washed

(Taken from 'Physical signs of sexual abuse in children' – a report of the Royal College of Physicians, London 1991, page 56.)[4]

P30, which is detected by the P30 ELISA technique.

In view of the fact that the physical changes of abuse heal extremely rapidly and semen evidence is soon lost, it is axiomatic that the detection rate will be improved by early examination. Forensic specimens should be carefully labelled and handling should be documented to maintain a 'chain of evidence'. The collection and interpretation of forensic evidence have recently been well reviewed by De Jong and Finkel.[3]

Sexually transmitted disease

Whenever abuse is suspected, tests to isolate a sexually transmitted disease should be performed. These may provide evidence of sexual abuse in the absence of physical signs. None of the sexually transmitted diseases is transmitted by fomites and only herpes simplex type 1 and syphilis are well documented as having a non-sexual mode of transmission. All the common sexually transmitted diseases have been documented as passing from mother to infant either before birth or during the birth process. Infection of the infant at birth may not be immediately apparent. When encountering perineal warts (condylomata acuminata) or chlamydial infection in a young child, cognisance should be given to the fact that such infection may have been acquired one to two years previously in the birth process. *Gardnerella vaginalis*, the organism most frequently implicated in bacterial vaginosis, is not commonly found in the vagina of prepubertal girls. Its isolation, however, does not necessarily prove sexual contact. Similarly, genital mycoplasmas which are found more commonly in abused girls are also found in normal girls.

There is now good evidence that human papillomavirus is sexually transmitted in children. Sexual abuse should always be seriously considered in children presenting with perineal warts after the age of two. However, cognisance should also be given to the large numbers of reports in the literature where anogenital warts have been reported without evidence of sexual abuse. The aetiology in many instances being due to autoinoculation or heteroinoculation.

Ideally warts should be biopsied and typed in a specialist laboratory in view of the oncogenic potential of certain human papillomavirus types (16, 18, 31). Children infected with these types need to be kept under review. In the UK, wart typing is usually not undertaken by laboratories as a service commitment, but may be carried out as part of an ongoing research programme. At present DNA typing is not sufficiently reliable to be used in a medico-legal arena.

Subsequent care of the sexually abused child

Children who have sustained genital injuries or acquired sexually transmitted diseases may need treatment. The expert advice of a gynaecologist or venereologist is well worth considering. In postpubertal girls when the abuse occurs in mid cycle it is necessary to give postcoital contraception within 72 hours of intercourse.

In the case of sexual assault children should be tested for syphylis and HIV (human immunodeficiency virus) three months after the incident. It may also be necessary to repeat cultures for sexually transmitted disease as cultures within hours of contact may fail to detect an early infection.

Measures to protect the child are normally initiated by the Social Services. The physician is expected to attend case conferences where information is shared with other professionals. Court appearance on behalf of the Local Authority or the police could be required. The subsequent emotional needs not only of the child but also of the whole family should not be forgotten. These are best addressed by close co-operation between the social worker and a child psychiatrist or psychologist.

In conclusion, the last decade has seen much progress in defining what is normal and the physical signs of abuse have been well documented. As in most areas of medicine this area is not free from controversy and pitfalls. Experience has shown that these can best be minimised by the physician working in close co-operation with other agencies. For further guidance readers are referred to two recently published authoritative reports (Report of the Royal College of Physicians 1991[4] and Statement of American Academy of Pediatrics 1991[5]).

References

1. De Jong AR, Rose M. Legal proof of child sexual abuse in the absence of physical evidence. *Pediatrics* 1991; **88**: 506–11.
2. Hobbs CJ, Wynne JM. Buggery in childhood – a common syndrome of child abuse. *Lancet* 1986; **ii**: 792–6.
3. De Jong AR, Finkel MA. Sexual abuse of children. *Current Problems in Pediatrics* 1990; **20**: 534–40.
4. Royal College of Physicians Report. *Physical Signs of Sexual Abuse in Children*. London: The Royal College of Physicians, 1991.
5. American Academy of Pediatrics. Guidelines for the evaluation of sexual abuse of children. *Pediatrics* 1991; **87**: 254–60.
6. Herman-Giddens ME, Frothingham TE. Prepubertal female genitalia: examination for evidence of sexual abuse. *Pediatrics* 1987; **80**: 203–8.
7. Neinstein LS, Goldenring J, Carpenter S. Nonsexual transmission of sexually transmitted diseases: an infrequent occurrence. *Pediatrics* 1984; **74**: 67–76.
8. Spencer MJ, Dunklee F. Sexual abuse of boys. *Pediatrics* 1986; **78**: 133–8.

9. Emans SJ, Woods ER, Flagg NT, Freeman A. Genital findings in sexually abused, symptomatic and asymptomatic girls. *Pediatrics* 1987; **79**: 778–85.

10. McCann J, Voris J, Simon M. Labial adhesions and posterior fourchette injuries in childhood sexual abuse. *American Journal of Diseases in Childhood* 1988; **142**: 659–63.

11. Muram D. Child sexual abuse – genital tract findings in prepubertal girls. *American Journal of Obstetric Gynecology* 1989; **160**: 328–32.

12. Muram D. Child sexual abuse: relationship between sexual acts and genital findings. *Child Abuse and Negligence* 1989; **13**: 211–16.

13. Muram D, Elias S. Child sexual abuse – genital tract findings in prepubertal girls. Comparison of colposcopic and unaided examinations. *American Journal of Obstetric Gynecology* 1989; **160**: 333–5.

14. West R, Davies A, Fenton T. Accidental vulval injuries in childhood. *British Medical Journal* 1989; **298**: 1002–3.

15. White S, Ingram DL, Lyna PR. Vaginal introital diameter in the evaluation of sexual abuse. *Child Abuse and Negligence* 1989; **13**: 217–24.

16. McCann, Voris J, Simon M, Wells R. Perianal findings in prepubertal children selected for nonabuse: a descriptive study. *Child Abuse and Negligence* 1989; **13**: 179–93.

17. Hobbs CJ, Wynne JM. Sexual abuse of English boys and girls: the importance of anal examination. *Child Abuse and Negligence* 1989; **13**: 195–210.

18. Herman-Giddens ME, Berson NL. Harmful genital care practices in children – a type of child abuse. *JAMA* 1989; **261**: 577–9.

19. Goff CW, Burke KR, Rickenback C, Buebendorf DP. Vaginal opening measurement in prepubertal girls. *American Journal of Diseases in Childhood* 1989; **143**: 1366–8.

20. Hammerschlag MR. Chlamydial infections. *Journal of Pediatrics* 1989; **114**: 727–34.

21. Davis JA, Emans SJ. Human papillomavirus infection in the pediatric and adolescent patient. *Journal of Pediatrics* 1989; **115**: 1–9.

22. Chadwick DL, Berkowitz CD, Kerns D, McCann J, Reinhart MA, Strickland S. *Colour Atlas of Child Sexual Abuse*. Chicago: Yearbook Medical Publishers, 1989.

23. Berth-Jones J, Graham-Brown RAC, Burns DA. Lichen sclerosis. *Archives of Disease in Childhood* 1989; **64**: 1204–6.

24. McCann J, Voris J, Simon M, Wells R. Comparison of genital examination techniques in prepubertal girls. *Pediatrics* 1990a; **85**: 182–7.

25. McCann J, Wells R, Simon M, Voris J. Genital findings in prepubertal girls selected for non-abuse: a descriptive study. *Pediatrics* 1990b; **86**: 428–39.

26. Heger A, Emans SJ. Introital diameter as the criterion for sexual abuse. *Pediatrics* 1990; **85**: 222–33.

27. Hobbs CJ, Wynne JM. The sexually abused battered child. *Archives of Disease in Childhood* 1990; **65**: 423–7.

28. Bays J, Jenny C. Genital and anal conditions confused with child sexual abuse. *American Journal of Disease in Childhood* 1990; **144**: 1319–22.

29. Berenson A, Heger A, Andrews S. Appearance of the hymen in newborns. *Pediatrics* 1991; **87**: 458–65.

30. Johnson CF. Prolapse of the urethra: confusion of clinical and anatomic characteristics with sexual abuse. *Pediatrics* 1991; **87**: 722–5.
31. Kellog ND, Parra JM. Linea vestibularis: a previously undescribed normal genital structure in female neonates. *Pediatrics*, 1991; **87**: 926–9.
32. Gabby T, Winkleby M, Boyce W, Fisher D, Lancaster A, Sensabough G, Crim D. Sexual abuse of children – the detection of semen on skin. *American Journal of Diseases in Childhood* 1992; **146**: 700–3.
33. Gardner J. Comparison of the vaginal flora in sexually abused and non-abused girls. *Journal of Pediatrics* 1992; **120**: 872–7.
34. Gutman LT, St Claire K, Herman-Giddens ME, Johnston WW, Phelps WC. Evaluation of sexually abused and non-abused young girls for intravaginal human papillomavirus infection. *American Journal of Diseases in Childhood* 1992; **146**: 694–9.
35. McCann J, Voris J, Simon M. Genital injuries resulting from sexual abuse: a longitudinal study. *Pediatrics* 1992; **89**: 307–17.
36. Pierce AM, Hart CA. Vulvovaginitis: causes and management. *Archives of Disease in Childhood* 1992; **67**: 509–12.
37. Berenson A, Heger A, Hayes J, Bailey R, Emans S. Appearance of the hymen in prepubertal girls. *Pediatrics* 1992; **89**: 387–94.
38. Kerns DL, Ritter ML, Thomas RG. Concave hymenal variations in suspected child abuse victims. *Pediatrics* 1992; **90**: 265–72.
39. Gutman LT, Herman-Giddens ME, Phelps WC. Transmission of human papilloma-virus disease: comparison of data from adults and children. *Pediatrics* 1993; **91**: 31–8.
40. McCann J, Voris J. Perianal injuries resulting from sexual abuse: a longitudinal study. *Pediatrics* 1993; **91**: 390–7.

15 Unusual manifestations of child abuse

In recent years there has been a profusion of reports of the most bizarre kind of child abuse. The methods employed are often so wanton, devious or extraordinary as to beggar the imagination. When dealing with such cases it is very important, in the interest of the child, that information be carefully documented as part of a thorough investigation. Unfortunately difficulty may be encountered in litigation because the courts find it hard to believe that anyone would be capable of carrying out such bizarre and egregious acts against a child. Many abusers are articulate, intelligent and very plausible, often creating a good impression by their appearance and manner, thus further stretching the bounds of credulity.

Some of the most sensational reports are those of children being drowned in bathtubs, intentionally burned in microwave ovens, or with a stun gun. With the current epidemic of cocaine abuse in the USA seizures from passive inhalation and injury from chemicals used in the purification process have been recorded. There is strong suspicion that coccaine has been administered to children.

The hair/fibre tourniquet syndrome is likely to be mistaken for an unusual form of abuse. Hair or garment fibres may become accidentally entwined around one or more digits or the penis, causing vascular occlusion. The compromised circulation results in swelling, oedema, ulceration and rarely gangrene. The unwary doctor encountering a child with a constriction of the digits or penis is likely to perceive the injury as abusive. There are, however, a number of reports in the literature attesting to these injuries being accidental.

Most of the literature concerning unusual abuse has focused on a condition known as 'Munchausen syndrome by proxy'.

Munchausen syndrome by proxy (MSP)

The term MSP was coined by Meadow in 1977 to describe a situation where a carer (usually the mother) creates factitious symptoms or signs in order to mislead the physician into believing the child is ill. Although there had been previous reports of such instances both in the English and French literature it was Meadow's seminal paper in the *Lancet* which was instrumental in galvanising interest in this phenomenon. Asher in 1951 coined the term 'Munchausen syndrome' after Baron von Munchausen, a man well known for his wide travels and mendacity. The syndrome described the behaviour pattern of adults who repeatedly got themselves admitted to hospital by falsifying signs and symptoms and creating a web of deception. The hallmarks of MSP are as follows:

1. Illness in a child is fabricated by a parent or someone who is *in loco parentis*.
2. The child is presented for medical assessment and care, usually persistently, often resulting in multiple medical procedures ('iatrogenic abuse').
3. The perpetrator denies the cause of the child's illness.
4. Acute signs and symptoms of illness cease when the child is separated from the perpetrator (invariably the mother).

The clinical spectrum

Children presenting with MSP are usually infants or of preschool age. The most common situation is for the mother to provide a false illness, factitious epilepsy being particularly common. For children in infancy doctors would be well advised to have fits confirmed by someone other than the mother before anticonvulsants are commenced. The mother may lie about family history or even about a serious illness having been diagnosed in another hospital. Furthermore, the situation may be confused by the mother who fabricates signs or adulterates investigation specimen samples. For this purpose she may add salt, sugar, chemicals or colouring agents. Her own blood or blood from raw meat may be added. The net result is biochemical chaos and obfuscation. Another 'trick' on the ward is for the child's samples to be swapped with those of another child with a genuine illness.

A wide variety of signs can be induced, involving most systems of the body. Skin signs may be induced by applying irritants or by rubbing (dermatitis artefacta). Diarrhoea, vomiting, neurological problems and biochemical disorders can be induced by covert administration of laxatives, emetics, sedatives, tranquillisers, salt and chemicals. Weight loss may be caused by interference with the child's nutrition while in hospital. Thermometers may be heated to produce fever or temperature charts altered. The signs and symptoms and biochemical changes may be so bizarre prompting the experienced physician to utter 'he has never seen a case like this before'. About three-quarters of these children have at least one of these additional features: a history of failure to thrive or neglect, non-accidental injury or inappropriate medication. There have been reports of factitious abuse (physical and sexual) in the context of MSP. Parents create the signs (e.g. enlarge the hymenal orifice with a finger or tampon) or coach the children in order to have the allegations substantiated. Children may be 'brainwashed' to such an extent that they are unable to distinguish reality from unreality.

Most mothers are intelligent, pleasant and co-operative and form a good relationship with medical and nursing staff. Fathers are generally minimally involved in the family and are absent for prolonged periods. Marital dysfunction is common. A minority of mothers spend little time on the ward which may make staff question the mother–child relationship. Most have an overclose relationship with the child. Many have a psychiatric history. Self-injury and drug overdose are common. A large number have been exposed to some form of abuse in childhood and behaviour problems in adolescence are frequent. Those that have been given a psychiatric diagnosis are said to have a 'personality disorder' or 'reactive depression'. The mothers' motivation for acting in this intriguing way is open to speculation. It might be a way of attracting sympathy and attention which would otherwise not be forthcoming.

The outlook for children subjected to MSP is poor, many will eventually collude with their mothers' fabrications and during adolescence develop hysterical conversion reactions and symptoms of Munchausen syndrome. The problem is clearly multigenerational. Psychotherapy is usually not very effective because of the persistent denial by the perpetrator. The outlook for siblings needs to be given careful consideration. In a recently reported retrospective study Bools et al found 11% (probably an underestimate) of siblings had died in early childhood, the cause of death not being identified. A large number had been abused, neglected, subjected to inappropriate medication and had fabricated illness. Given the known mortality, psychological and physical morbidity, evidence that siblings are often similarly abused, the sophistication of the abuser, level of denial, and intractability to treatment, there needs to be extreme caution in allowing these children to remain in the custody of the perpetrator. Reporting of such cases to Social Services is mandatory. It needs to be emphasised that much valuable information about the family background, both medical and social, can be obtained by close communication between the hospital physician and the general practitioner.

Many physicians now regard suffocation and poisoning as a variant of MSP. Children suffering these forms of abuse could be said to be undergoing 'gentle battering' in that unlike their physically abused counterparts there is seldom evidence of abuse.

Suffocation

There are now a number of reports of children who have been deliberately suffocated by smothering. Such scenes of smothering have been secretly captured on videotape in hospital and covert cameras are now used in some hospitals as a means of proving the diagnosis. This method, however, lacks sensitivity as mothers who might suffocate their children at home may not do so during hospital admission.

Smothering may be done impulsively when the mother feels violent towards the child or it may be perpetrated in a repetitive, systematic way. It usually starts between the first and third month and continues for months or years until the child dies or it is detected. Children may present with 'near miss cot death', recurrent episodes of unexplained apnoea/cyanotic episodes or seizures. The younger child is more likely to be diagnosed as having apnoea and the older child seizures. Seizures are notoriously resistant to anticonvulsants. If the child is admitted to hospital characteristically these episodes do not occur when there is no parental presence. When a parent is present resuscitation will invariably be initiated by the parent.

There is definite evidence that a *very small* number of cot deaths, particularly recurrent deaths in the same family, are caused by filicide (child homicide caused by either parent). Smothering an infant may be accomplished without any anatomic injury. Placing a hand, pillow or item of clothing over the infant's mouth and nose until he/she dies may produce minor abrasions or contusions of the face or buccal mucosa, and evidence of such pressure should be diligently sought in every unexplained death in infancy. It is, however, possible to smother a baby without a trace of physical evidence. Likewise, placing a foreign object such as a tissue or sock down the throat may cause no demonstrable evidence if the obstruction is removed prior to the examination. Chest compression (traumatic asphyxia) may also leave no marks. Facial petechia, commonly found in asphyxia, particularly with thoracic compression, may be absent. Suspicion of smothering should be aroused when a *combination* of factors is present. These are age greater than six months, previous sibling death, history of apnoea/cyanotic episodes and an unexplained disorder. Where the length of suffocation is not prolonged children may not succumb but sustain brain damage.

The psychological profile of parents is similar to that of MSP. A higher incidence of eating disorders (anorexia and obesity) has been reported. Unlike MSP parents do not intentionally seek out a number of different specialists. Denial is just as common but when caught in the act on videotape they are more likely to confess. It differs from 'classical' MSP in that there are reports of fathers who smother their infants.

Poisoning

Children are poisoned with a variety of drugs and common household substances. Sedatives and tranquillisers are the drugs most commonly used. The wide use of these drugs in society renders easy access to them. They may cause seizures, coma and other unexplained neurological signs. There are reports of children poisoned with pepper which has proved fatal when aspirated. Generally the pouring of pepper into the child's mouth has been employed as a form of chastisement. Similarly there are many reports of salt ingestion, excess water consumption and water deprivation (not strictly poisoning). Deviations from normal salt and water consumption create electrolyte chaos. Children are sometimes fed alcohol or forced to drink it. In a review of poisoned children Dine and McGovern found 20% had been abused and in 30% poisoning continued while the child was in hospital.

Poisoned children are usually less than three and the physician should be alerted to poisoning by the following features:

1. Inexplicable signs, symptoms and biochemical values.
2. Neurological signs of acute onset such as ataxia, seizures and coma.
3. Episodic illness.
4. Relationship between timing of episodes and parental visits.
5. Child normal in hospital but recurrence after discharge.
6. Unexplained illness, injury or death in a sibling.

Should poisoning be suspected it is worth doing an abdominal x-ray. Where ingestion is recent certain radio-opaque drugs and crystals such as salt or sugar may be apparent. There is often an overclose relationship between mother and child, and like MSP there is frequently a psychiatric history, a history of drug overdose or marital disharmony.

The diagnosis can be proved by detecting the drug in blood, urine or gastric contents. Most hospitals provide a 'toxins screen' which is limited to the common drugs only. A specific assay can be arranged by contacting a Poisons Unit such as that at New Cross Hospital, London. The decision about which assay to request is dependent upon the signs and symptoms and the types of drugs available in the home. Medical details of the inhabitants of the household may be required. A quick telephone call to the general practitioner often proves invaluable in these circumstances. Physicians would also be well advised to discuss the case with a consultant at the Poisons Unit. Where suspicion of poisoning is strong the police should be contacted and they will arrange for an assay at a Home Office forensic laboratory. Where there is no police involvement specimens should be carefully labelled with the name, date and time and signed for at each stage of transfer to the Poisons Unit so as to establish a 'chain of evidence'. The correct handling of specimens could prove vital should any legal action ensue. Deaths due to poisoning, like all deaths arising out of child abuse, are the concern of the coroner. Should any physician have a suspicion of child death by poisoning the coroner should be informed.

In the UK and Eire there are eight Poison Information Centres. They will provide round-the-clock information and advice to physicians caring for poisoned children. They will also assist in identifying a toxin. The names and telephone numbers of these centres are shown below:

Belfast	0232 240503
Birmingham	021 554 3801
Cardiff	0222 709901
Dublin	010 3531 379966
Edinburgh	031 229 2477
Leeds	0532 430715
London	071 635 9191
Newcastle	091 232 5131

Further reading

Unusual manifestations

1. Narcewicz RM. Distal digital occlusion. *Pediatrics* 1978; **61**: 922–3.
2. Oates RK. Overturning the diagnosis of child abuse. *Archives of Disease in Childhood* 1984; **59**: 665–7.
3. Johnson CF. Constricting bands. Manifestations of possible child abuse. *Clinical Pediatrics* 1988; **27**: 439–44.
4. Frechette A, Rimza ME. Stun Gun injury: a new presentation of the battered child syndrome. *Pediatrics* 1992; **89**: 898–901.
5. Kemp AM, Matt AM, Sibert JR. Accidents and child abuse in bathtub submersions. *Archives of Disease in Childhood* 1994; **70**: 435–438.

Munchausen syndrome by proxy

1. Asher R. Munchausen's syndrome. *Lancet* 1951; **1**: 339–41.
2. Meadow R. Munchausen syndrome by proxy: hinterland of child abuse. *Lancet* 1977; **2**: 343–5.
3. Meadow R. Management of Munchausen syndrome by proxy. *Archives of Disease in Childhood* 1985; **60**: 385–93.
4. Rosenberg DA. Web of deceit: a literature review of Munchausen syndrome by proxy. *Child Abuse and Neglect* 1987; **11**: 547–63.
5. McGuire TL, Feldman KW. Psychologic morbidity of children subjected to Munchausen syndrome by proxy. *Pediatrics* 1989; **83**: 289–92.
6. Sneed RC. Breed or Meadow? – Munchausen or Münchausen. *Pediatrics* 1989; **83**: 1078.

7. Alexander R, Smith W, Stevenson R. Serial Munchausen syndrome by proxy. *Pediatrics* 1990; **86**: 581–5.
8. Bools CN, Neale BA, Meadow SR. Co-morbity associated with fabricated illness (Munchausen syndrome by proxy). *Archives of Disease in Childhood* 1992; **67**: 77–9.
9. Samuels MP, Southall DP. Munchausen syndrome by proxy. *British Journal of Hospital Medicine* 1992; **47**: 759–62.
10. Meadow R. False allegations of abuse and Munchausen syndrome by proxy. *Archives of Disease in Childhood* 1993; **68**: 444–7.

Suffocation

1. Rosen CL, Frost JD, Glaze DG. Child abuse and recurrent infant apnoea. *Journal of Pediatrics* 1986; **109**: 1065–7.
2. Williams C, Bevan VT. The secret observation of children in hospital. *Lancet* 1988; **1**: 780–1.
3. Meadow R. Suffocation, recurrent apnoea and sudden infant death. *Journal of Pediatrics* 1990; **117**: 351–7.
4. Makar AF, Squier PJ. Munchausen syndrome by proxy: father as a perpetrator. *Pediatrics* 1990; **85**: 370–3.
5. Samuels MP, McClaughlin W, Jacobson RR, Poets CF, Southall DP. Fourteen cases of imposed upper airway obstruction. *Archives of Disease in Childhood* 1992; **67**: 162–70.
6. Anon. Diagnosing recurrent suffocation of children. *Lancet* 1992; **340**: 87.
7. Anon. Spying on mother. *Lancet* 1994; **343**: 1373–74.

Poisoning

1. Rogers D, Tripp J, Bentovim A, Robinson A, Berry D, Goulding R. Non-accidental poisoning: an extended syndrome of child abuse. *British Medical Journal* 1976; **1**: 793–6.
2. Dine MS, McGovern ME. Intentional poisoning of children – an overlooked category of child abuse: report of seven cases and review of the literature. *Pediatrics* 1982; **70**: 32–5.
3. Kharasch S, Vinci R, Reece R. Esophagitis, epiglottitis, and cocaine alkaloid ('Crack'): 'accidental' poisoning or child abuse. *Pediatrics* 1990; **86**: 117–19.
4. Reece RM. Unusual manifestations of child abuse. *Pediatric Clinics of North America* 1990; **37**: 905–21.
5. Dockery KW. Fatal intentional salt poisoning associated with a radio-opaque mass. *Pediatrics* 1992; **89**: 964–5.
6. Meadow R. Non-accidental salt poisoning. *Archives of Disease in Childhood* 1993; **68**: 448–52.

16   The Children Act 1989

The Children Act 1989 is the most comprehensive piece of legislation enacted about children. It replaces previously fragmented pieces of legislation with a composite statement of the law relating to the care and protection of children. The Act brings together for the first time public and private law relating to children. Briefly, public law deals with those areas where society intervenes in the actions of individuals (such as care proceedings) and private law addresses the behaviour of individuals to each other (such as with whom children should reside following a divorce).

The origins of child care legislation in Britain date back a century. Ferguson has written:

> In the 1880s, reformers and social workers developed a systematic legal and social child protection practice in response to what they regarded as a major problem of child abuse. By 1908, in the Children Act of that year, a specific child protection practice had been codified and institutionalised into the foundation of the modern welfare state.

In the last 20 years, as one child abuse Public Inquiry followed another, it became patently clear that children's law was in need of an overhaul. Following the death of Maria Collwell in 1973 and until the Cleveland sex abuse Inquiry in 1987, a groundswell of opinion for change in the law had developed. Public opinon, together with two seminal reviews highlighting deficiencies in the law, were instrumental in the enactment of the Children Act 1989.

In 1985 the Social Services Select Committee produced 'A Review of Child Care Law' which looked at a number of shortcomings in public law, specifically the legislative basis of statutory intervention such as child protection and care proceedings. The second review published by the Law Commission in 1988 entitled 'Review of Child Care Law: Guardianship and Custody' looked at private law, specifically disputes between private individuals over matters such as custody arrangements after divorce.

The *Gillick* case in 1986 had a profound effect on the drafting of legislation and the way the law now relates to responsible children under 16. The *Gillick* case (about contraception) was a landmark in that the Law Lords established a point of law. It recognised for the first time the views of children under 16 who were of sufficient intelligence, understanding and maturity. Such children are now colloquially known as 'Gillick competent'.

The main principles of the Act can be summarised as follows:

1. The welfare of the child is paramount.
2. Children are best looked after within the family, parents playing a full part without resort to the law.
3. Court orders should only be made if it is better than making no order at all.
4. Emphasis is given to the avoidance of delay in the resolution of court proceedings concerning the welfare of the child.
5. The courts and agencies should give due consideration to race, culture, religion and language.
6. Children should participate in decisions about their care and should be kept informed of decisions.
7. Parents with 'children in need' should be helped to bring up the children themselves. This help should be provided by the agencies in partnership with the parents. Intrusion into family life should be kept to a minimum.
8. Parents have parental responsibility for their children even when their children are no longer living with them. When a child is in care (Local Authority) parental responsibility is shared with the parents but the Local Authority is the final arbiter in deciding how that responsibility is exercised.

What is meant by 'children in need'?

The Act (Section 17(10)) defines children in need as follows:

(a) He is unlikely to achieve or maintain, or have the opportunity of achieving or maintaining, a reasonable standard of health or development without the provision for him of services by a local authority;
(b) his health or development is likely to be significantly impaired, or further impaired without the provision for him of such services; or
(c) he is disabled.

What is parental responsibility (PR)?

The Act (Section 3(1)) states parental responsibility 'means all the rights, duties, powers, responsibilities and authority which by law a parent of a child has in relation to the child and his property'. The Act does not, however, define what the 'rights, duties, powers, responsibilities and authority' are in relation to appropriate parenting. The mother of the child automatically has PR as does a married father (Section 2(2)). An unmarried father may acquire it through application to the court, or on a prescribed form without going to court if the mother agrees. He may also acquire it by an appointment made in the construction of a will.

A person who has parental responsibility may not surrender it or transfer any part of it, but may arrange for some or all of it to be met by one or more persons acting on his behalf (a private arrangement – Section 2(9)). It can also be conferred by a court in making out a Care Order or Residence Order or awarding guardianship in the case of parental death (Section 5(1)).

Parental responsibility will diminish as the child acquires sufficient understanding to make his/her own decisions. Parental responsibility is lost by a natural parent in the case of adoption. It should be noted that not having parental responsibility does not absolve an unmarried father from any financial liability (Section 3(4)).

Children Act Court Orders (Parts IV and V) are most pertinent to child abuse and the protection of children, and a brief overview of the various orders will be provided. The Act (Section 47(1)) specifies that if a Local Authority is informed or has reasonable cause to suspect that the child is suffering or is likely to suffer significant harm, 'the Authority shall make, or cause to be made, such enquiries as it considers necessary to enable it to decide whether it should take any action to safeguard or promote the child's welfare'. It is the duty of the Health Authority or Trust, any Local Authority, education or housing authority or NSPCC to assist enquiries by providing relevant information and advice unless it would be unreasonable to do so (Section 47(9) and (11)).

What is meant by 'significant harm'?

Harm includes both:

(a) ill-treatment (which includes sexual abuse and non-physical ill-treatment such as emotional abuse), and
(b) the impairment of health or development: health means physical or mental health; development means physical, intellectual, emotional, social or behavioural development (Section 31(9)).

'Significant' impairment of health or development in this context requires comparison with the health or development which could be expected from a similar child with similar attributes and needs (Section 31(10)).

Child protection (Part V)

The Emergency Protection Order (EPO) (Section 44)

Application for this order can be made by anyone to a court or individual magistrate. The effect is to give the applicant parental responsibility and the right to remove the child or prevent the child from being removed. If, during the time period of an EPO, the applicant has reason to believe that the child's safety would be assured if the child returned to the home or left the 'place of safety' the applicant should proceed with such arrangements. Should the circumstances change within the time limit of the EPO and the child is again deemed to be at risk of significant harm the EPO can be reactivated.

For an Emergency Protection Order to be granted a court must be satisfied that there is reasonable cause to believe that the child is likely to suffer 'significant harm' if not removed to accommodation provided by the applicant or does not remain in his current location (e.g. a hospital). An EPO may also be granted if the court is satisfied that Local Authority or NSPCC investigation of risk is being thwarted by unreasonable refusal of access. Identification will need to be provided by the officer of the Local Authority or NSPCC.

The duration of an EPO is eight days with one possible extension of a further seven days (Section 45). If the last day of an eight day order falls on a public holiday (Christmas, Good Friday, a Bank Holiday or Sunday) the court may specify a period which ends at noon on the first later day which is not a public holiday. Unless the parents were given notice and attended the hearing they are entitled to make an application for discharge of the EPO after 72 hours. Such an application can be made by anyone with parental responsibility or with whom the child was residing at the time of the EPO or by the child himself. During the duration of the EPO reasonable contact between the child and his parents is assumed, and can only be restricted by a court direction.

The court will consider the appointment of a guardian ad litem at the application stage. What is familiarly called 'hearsay' evidence will be admissible (Section 45(7)). Medical or psychiatric examination may be required while the EPO is in place and the child is being assessed. A child may refuse to undergo an assessment provided he is of sufficient understanding to comprehend the consequences of his refusal. The court may direct that an applicant exercising any powers he has by virtue of the order be accompanied by a doctor, nurse or health visitor, if he so chooses. If necessary a court may direct someone to disclose to the applicant the whereabouts of a child (Section 48(1)). It should, however, be noted that a statement or admission made in complying with the court direction to disclose the child's whereabouts is not admissible in evidence against him or his spouse in any proceedings other than perjury. This privilege against incrimination applies to Part IV and V Orders.

An EPO may also include directions to enter and search (Section 48(3)). Where the court believes an applicant has been or is likely to be refused access to a child it may issue a warrant to the police to assist, using reasonable force if necessary (Section 48(9) and (10)).

What is a guardian ad litem?

Under the Act in the vast majority of public law cases the court will appoint a guardian ad litem (GAL). Such a person is an independent social worker who will represent the child's interest in the proceedings. As a court-appointed independent representative of the child the GAL plays an important part in providing a link between the child, the court and the various multidisciplinary agencies involved with the case. The GAL has specific powers and duties set out in Rules of Court, which include appointing a solicitor to act for the child. A written report containing a recommendation about the best outcome for the child is submitted by the GAL to the court. The GAL has a legal right to see and make copies of Social Services records (Section 42). There is no right of access of Health Authority records except insofar as they form part of Social Services records. The GAL is entitled to attend child protection case conferences as an observer not a participant. Attendance at the conference will assist information gathering.

Police Power of Protection (PPOP) (Section 46)

This allows a police constable to remove a child or ensure that he remains in his current location (e.g. a hospital). It allows the police to do all that is reasonable, but does not give the police parental responsibility. The grounds for Police Power of Protection are that the child would otherwise suffer 'significant harm'. The police must inform those with parental responsibility, the child (if of sufficient understanding) and the Local Authority of the steps taken (Section 46(3) and (4)) and the child should be transferred as soon as possible to Local Authority accommodation. The duration of a PPOP is a maximum of 72 hours (Section 46(6)). The contact provisions are different from an Emergency Protection Order in that the 'designated police officer' (person designated by the Chief Constable) *must* allow contact with others as in the opinion of the officer is both reasonable and in the child's best interests (Section 46(10)). While a child is in police protection the police may apply for an EPO on behalf of the Local Authority, whether or not the Local Authority knows of it or agrees to it (Section 46(8)). Any time in police protection must be deducted from time on an EPO.

Recovery Order (Section 50)

Such an order is made when a child who is subject to an EPO, PPOP or

Care Order (including Interim Care Order) runs away from or is kept from the responsible adult who should be caring for him. Applications for such orders are generally made by the Local Authority, NSPCC or police. This order directs the relevant person to produce the child or inform of the child's whereabouts. It authorises the police to search (using reasonable force if necessary) and allows removal of the child by the authorised person.

If a child subject to one of these orders is accepted into the home of a foster parent or a Registered or Voluntary Home they will be exempt from prosecution provided they have a certificate issued by the Secretary of State. The intention is to permit so-called 'safe houses' which operate as refuges for children who run or stay away from home to be free from potential prosecution provided that they act in accordance with the regulations. One of these requirements is that the person running the refuge must notify the police on reception of the child (Section 51).

Child Assessment Order (CAO) (Section 43)

Application for this order can be made by the Local Authority or NSPCC. The applicant must satisfy the court that:

1. there is reasonable cause to suspect that the child is suffering or likely to suffer significant harm and
2. assessment of health or development needs to be made to determine whether the child is suffering significant harm or is likely to suffer significant harm and
3. such an assessment is otherwise unlikely to be undertaken or be satisfactory.

The effect of this order is that it forces the person(s) to produce the child and ensures compliance with the directions of the court (for example a medical examination). If a child is of sufficient understanding or 16 or more, assessment may be refused. It remains to be seen whether the courts would override a child's refusal of consent for examination or assessment. The maximum duration of a CAO is seven days (no extension) and if necessary a child may be kept from home.

Care and supervision (Part IV)

Applications for such orders, like the orders previously discussed, are made by the Local Authority or NSPCC to the Family Proceedings Court (magistrates' court). Proceedings likely to last more than two days are then referred to the county court. Appeals about making or refusal to make an order are referred to the High Court (Family Division). The court will only make an order if it is satisfied that it is better than making no order at all (Section 1(5)). It will need to be satisfied that the child (up to 17th birthday, or 16th if married) is

(a) suffering or likely to suffer significant harm and
(b) that harm or likelihood of harm is attributable to
    (i)   the care given to the child, or likely to be given to him if the order were not made, not being what it would be reasonable to expect a parent to give to him: or
    (ii) the child being beyond parental control.

Care order

This lasts until the child is 18 and gives the Local Authority parental responsibility and the right to decide to what extent parents can meet their continuing parental responsibility. It discharges any existing order, and if the child is a ward of court, the wardship. The Act assumes 'reasonable contact' with parents, any guardian, any person holding a Residence Order when the Care Order was made, or a person having care of the child by virtue of a High Court Order. The Local Authority can apply to court for an order which limits or refuses contact with the above persons. Before making a Care Order (including Interim Order), the court must consider the arrangements which the Authority has made, or proposes to make, for affording any person contact with the child and should invite the parties to comment on these arrangements (Section 34(11)). The Local Authority has a duty to consider the wishes, feelings, religion, race and cultural and linguistic background of the child and can withhold contact for a maximum of seven days if the matter is urgent and the child's welfare needs to be safeguarded (Section 34(6)). If no application for contact has been made and the court feels such an order should be made it has the power to make such an order (Section 34(5)).

Supervision Order (SO) (Section 35, Schedule 3, Parts I and II)

A Supervision Order lasts 12 months. It can be changed to a Care Order through the court or discharged. It can also be renewed to a maximum of three years.

It requires the supervisor to advise, assist and befriend the child and 'to take such steps as are reasonably necessary to give effect to the order'. It imposes obligations on the 'responsible person' (i.e. the person with parental responsibility or with whom the child is residing) to take steps to ensure compliance with the directions of the order. There is nothing explicit in the Act about what is involved in supervising. The court can through the order direct that the child receive medical or psychiatric treatment (not without consent in the case of children of sufficient understanding). It should be noted that when a court dismisses an application or grants an application for discharge it may make a 'pending appeal' Care Order/Supervision Order which may include specific directions to safeguard the child.

Interim orders

Interim Care and Supervision Orders may be made where there are 'reasonable grounds' so that an assessment can be undertaken prior to deciding whether a full Care or Supervision Order is required. The first Interim may be up to eight weeks. Second and subsequent Interims may be up to four weeks or the balance of the original eight weeks, if that is longer. Contact rights in Interim Care Orders are the same as a full Care Order and any challenge would be in accordance with Section 34 of the Act.

Application for variation and discharge of a Care Order or Supervision Order can be made by:

1. the person with parental responsibility,
2. the child,
3. Local Authority (supervisor in case of a Supervision Order) (Section 39).

Where an application has been made and it has been refused no further application can be made within six months without leave of the court (Section 91(17)).

Part II Orders (Section 8)

These orders are primarily concerned with 'private' law but can form part of any family proceedings. 'Family proceedings' are defined in effect as matrimonial and adoption proceedings on the one hand, and proceedings for Care or Supervision Order on the other.

The orders are:

Contact Order – requires the person with whom the child lives or is to live, to allow the child to visit or stay with, or otherwise have contact with the person named in the order.

Prohibited Steps Order – specifies steps that cannot be taken by a parent in exercising parental responsibility other than through obtaining the consent of the court.

Residence Order – made to settle with whom a child should live. It can be made in favour of more than one person. The person with whom the child lives has parental responsibility and cancels any existing Care Order.

Specific Issue Order – an order giving directions to resolve a particular problem that has arisen or may arise in connection with any aspect of parental responsibility for the child.

A court will not grant a Specific Issue or Prohibited Steps Order if a Residence or Contact Order would achieve the same result (Section 9). A court in Family Proceedings can make a Section 8 Order even if no application has been received. A Local Authority cannot apply for a Residence or Contact Order nor may these be made in its favour. It can apply for a Prohibited Steps or Specific Issue Order for a child being cared for by a parent or other care giver as well as for an 'accommodated' (voluntary care) child. Where a child is accommodated or in care any person who has the consent of the Local Authority may apply for a Residence Order. A parent, Guardian or Residence Order holder is entitled to apply for any Section 8 Order (Section 10).

Before concluding this section on the Children Act mention should be made of the Criminal Justice Act 1988, as amended by the 1991 Act, which makes substantial changes to the way in which children's evidence may be received by courts in criminal proceedings. An interview with a child may be video recorded and used as the main evidence in criminal proceedings subject to certain conditions. The Home Office, in conjunction with the Department of Health, has produced a document entitled *Memorandum of Good Practice*. It provides specific guidance on equipment and the production and storage of a video for court purposes.

Under the Act a video recording is acceptable in the Crown Court or Youth Court as evidence in chief in certain violent and sexual offences. The respective age limits are 14 for violent offences and 17 for sexual offences. It must be emphasised that this does not absolve the child from attendance at court as he would need to be available for cross-examination. For attendance to be waived the court would need to be satisfied that there were exceptional circumstances. Such circumstances are set out in the Criminal Justice Act 1988. Under the 1991 Act the child will be eligible to apply to give evidence from outside the courtroom via a live television link. At present such facilities are only available in Crown courts. Punctillious attention to the rules of evidence should be given to the making of a video as the courts have the power to edit or reject it should they consider it detrimental to a fair trial. Video recordings can also be used in civil proceedings should their use be required.

The 1991 Act was responsible for a fundamental change in the law as it relates to the competence of a child as a witness. Before the Act young children were assumed to be incompetent unless the contrary was proved. Competence needed to be established by satisfying the court that the child was of sufficient understanding to know the difference between truth and lies when giving evidence. Under the 1991 Act the child is assumed to be competent and there is now no longer a duty to examine the child as to competency before the trial. In certain circumstances as with adults it may be necessary to test for competency if the child is unable to give an understandable account of his evidence.

An information pack to lessen the courtroom trauma for abused children was launched by the Lord Chancellor in May 1993. The pack comprises two booklets for children aged five to nine and ten to 15 and an information leaflet for parents. It is intended to demystify the court process, correct misconceptions and make children more effective witnesses. The five to nine year olds' book includes a mock courtroom where children can put cardboard figures of the judge, witnesses and lawyers in their correct places. Children are told that their job in court is to listen carefully to the questions, answer them and tell the truth. Parents are warned that coaching or rehearsing the child could lead the prosecution to drop the case.

Further reading

1. Gillick v. West Norfolk and Wisbech Area Health Authority and Another (1986) AC 112, (1986) 1 FLR 224.
2. An introduction to the Children Act 1989. London: Her Majesty's Stationery Office, 1989.
3. Bridge J, Bridge S, Luke S. *Blackstone's Guide to the Children Act 1989*. London: Blackstone Press Limited, 1990.
4. Kent P, Pierson J, Thornton B. *Guide to the Children Act 1989*. Supplement to Community Care, 1990.
5. *Working Together under the Children Act 1989*. London: Her Majesty's Stationery Office, 1991.
6. Bainham A. Children – the New law – the Children Act 1989. Bristol: Jordan & Sons Ltd (Family Law), 1991.
7. Ferguson H. Rethinking child protection practices: a case for history. In: *The Violence Against Children Study Group, Taking Child Abuse Seriously*. (The study of welfare), London: Routledge, 1989.
8. *Memorandum of Good Practice*. London: Her Majesty's Stationery Office, 1992.
9. Mitchels B, Prince A. *The Children Act and Medical Practice*. Bristol: Jordan and Sons Ltd (Family Law), 1992.

17 Child abuse procedures – questions and answers

What is the Area Child Protection Committee (ACPC)?

The ACPC is a committee of professionals representing all the main authorities and agencies in the area which are involved in the prevention and management of child abuse. It is chaired by a senior member of Social Services (Assistant Director or above). Members express the views of the organisation to which they are accountable. The main function of the ACPC is the establishment of procedural guidelines for the prevention, management and monitoring of child abuse in each area. By the nature of its composition the ACPC ensures close co-operation between agencies and is responsible for inter-agency training. It undertakes reviews of deaths caused by child abuse as well as matters of child protection likely to be of public interest. It is the duty of the ACPC to prepare an annual report about local child abuse matters.

What is the Child Protection Case Conference?

It is a forum in which inter-agency professionals exchange information about a child and his/her family. A risk assessment is made and if necessary a child protection plan formulated. The only decision that need be made at the conference is whether the child's name should be placed on the Child Protection Register. Recommendations can be made to the Local Authority to instigate legal proceedings or to the police to pursue an investigation. Where a child is placed on the register a child protection plan will be formulated and a key worker (a social worker) appointed. It is the responsibility of the key worker to work closely with the family and to liaise with the various agencies in order to ensure that the protection plan is adhered to.

The agenda for the conference will vary from area to area and will depend on the circumstances of the case. In general the format of the discussion will be as follows:

1. Current concern about the child.
2. Any previous concern about the child or family.

3. Background information on family members and relationships. The police and the general practitioner are asked for information at this point.
4. The current social situation. Such matters as housing, employment, etc. are discussed.
5. Assessment of future risk of abuse (if any) and institution of protection plan (if necessary).
6. Summary of the conference decisions and recommendations and delegation of an individual who will convey this information to the family. The information is also subsequently sent to the family in writing.

When the abuse is deemed to be severe enough, the conference may recommend that application be made on behalf of the child to the Criminal Injuries Compensation Board.

Who calls the case conference and when is it held?

The conference is convened by the organisations with statutory powers (Local Authority or NSPCC (National Society for Prevention of Cruelty to Children)). Any concerned professional can ask the Local Authority (or NSPCC) to convene a conference. It is policy for a conference to be convened when an incident of abuse is suspected or confirmed whether or not future risk of abuse is adjudged to be minimal by an individual professional or agency. It is recommended that case conferences be held within eight working days of referral (maximum 15 days). The court process may require an early conference while investigation is being undertaken. The prime consideration in the timing of the conference is that all information should be to hand so that an informed decision can be made about the child's protection. At an early stage parents are informed orally and in writing of the timing of the conference and the procedure.

Which professionals attend the conference?

It is customary to invite all agencies which have responsibility in the child protection process. Such agencies include:

1. The Health Authority/Trust (paediatrician invited).
2. General practitioner.
3. Health visiting service.
4. Probation service.
5. Police.
6. Education service (when the child is of school age).
7. Appropriate voluntary organisations.

8. Social Services.
9. NSPCC (when operational in the area).

Some agencies are represented by more than one individual. Other professionals may be invited by the chair as the circumstances warrant. A member of the Local Authority legal department usually attends as his/her advice may be required about legal proceedings. The chair is taken by a senior manager of the Social Services Department (or NSPCC). Line managers who have been, or are likely to be, involved in decisions about the case should not chair conferences.

Can parents attend the conference?

In some areas provision has been made for parents to attend the whole or part of the conference. Other areas do not permit parental attendance, the rationale being that parental presence would inhibit the free flow of information, which would not be in the child's best interest. Parents have the right to have their views put to the conference and should be told how this can be done. Their views can be represented by letter, tape recording or through a professional at the meeting.

What information should be taken to the conference?

Some agencies prepare written reports for the conference which are read at the start. Doctors providing information at the conference should take the casenotes, x-rays, growth charts and photographs (if available). All agencies should collect information which should be prepared for presentation. The information provided by the doctor at the conference may form the basis for legal proceedings. Diligence is required in the presentation of that evidence as the doctor would be expected to present the same evidence to a court. Agencies or professionals unable to attend should send a report to the conference.

Information (including reports) presented to the conference is confidential. Notes are taken by the conference secretary who will prepare the minutes which are then despatched to each agency represented at the conference. Agencies are invited to highlight any inaccuracy in the minutes as soon as possible. The minutes are confidential and should be securely stored and not passed to a third person without the consent of the chair.

Is it possible to have a pre-birth case conference?

Yes, when there is sufficient concern about the risk to an unborn child such a conference can be convened. Parents or carers should be kept informed and should be involved in planning for the child's future. The conference may recommend placement of the child's name on the register at birth.

Can an appeal be made against the conference decision?

It should be emphasised that the case conference must not be perceived as a quasi-legal tribunal from which a right of appeal might be expected. Nevertheless, if a parent, family member or professional has strong feelings about the decision to register or not a formal letter of appeal should be sent to the Local Authority. The 'appeals procedure' as designated by the local ACPC will then ensue. It is unlikely that a professional would appeal as there is ample time at the conference (generally 60-90 minutes) for the expression of dissent and such dissent would be minuted.

Is it ethical for a doctor to divulge confidential information to the conference?

The view of the General Medical Council in this matter is unequivocal. An excerpt from the Annual Report in 1987 reads as follows:

> Both the British Medical Association and the medical defence societies have expressed the view that in such circumstances the interests of the child are paramount and that those interests may well override the general rule of professional confidence. On the recommendation of the Standards Committee, the Council in November 1987 expressed the view that, if a doctor has reason for believing that a child is being physically or sexually abused, not only is it permissible for the doctor to disclose information to a third party but it is a duty of a doctor to do so.

Unlike a court a doctor cannot be forced to attend a case conference. Attendance fees are payable to general practitioners and most hospital doctors. Details of these fees can be obtained from the British Medical Association.

What is the Child Protection Register?

It is a register maintained by Social Services in each Local Authority which lists children who are suffering from, or are likely to suffer from, significant harm and for whom there is a protection plan. The register provides a central point for quick inquiry about a child for whom there is concern and who may be subject to an inter-agency protection plan. The register is also used for statistical purposes and by the ACPC in policy development and strategic planning.

Children are only placed on the register after a case conference or when transferring from another area when already on the register in that area. Criteria for registration as set out in the inter-agency document 'Working Together' are as follows:

One of the following requirements needs to be satisfied:

1. There must be one or more identifiable incidents which can be described as having adversely affected the child. They may be acts of commission or omission. They can be either physical, sexual, emotional or neglectful. It is important to identify a specific occasion or occasions when the incident has occurred. Professional judgement is that further incidents are likely; or
2. Significant harm is expected on the basis of professional judgement or the investigation in this individual case or on research evidence.

Registration is categorised according to the type of abuse (neglect, physical injury, emotional and sexual abuse). Many children are categorised as suffering from more than one type of abuse. Where the criteria have been met with regard to an individual child and there is concern for other children in the household these children are usually also registered. Registration requires that the inter-agency protection plan be reviewed (review conference) at intervals of not more than six months. The first review conference is usually much sooner than six months. Review conferences are conducted by Social Services management in conjunction with the key worker. Other agencies are invited and asked to contribute. Any concerned professional may ask the Local Authority (or NSPCC) to call a review conference if it is believed that the child is not adequately protected or when there is a need for a change to the child protection plan. At every review conference the need for deregistration should be considered. If, for whatever reason, the child is no longer considered to be at risk he/she is deregistered. When a child is removed from the register the views of the participants of the review conference are carefully minuted and the minutes of the meeting as well as confirmation of removal of the name and any subsequent plans are confirmed in writing to all participants. It needs emphasising that a decision to deregister does not automatically lead to cessation of services. Discussion should take place with the parents and the child (if old enough) about future services that could be provided to assist the family following deregistration.

Further reading

1. *Working Together under the Children Act 1989. A Guide to Arrangements*

for Inter-agency Co-operation for the Protection of Children from Abuse. London: Her Majesty's Stationery Office, 1991.
2. *Child Abuse. A Study of Inquiry Reports 1980–1989.* London: Her Majesty's Stationery Office, 1991.

18   The doctor as a witness

Doctors working with abused children are required to provide reports and to attend court (Criminal and Family) as professional or expert witnesses. The difference between a professional witness and an expert is that an expert gives evidence of fact *and* opinion. Professional evidence is evidence of fact only. The Oxford Companion to Law describes expert evidence as 'evidence given to a Court by a person skilled and experienced in some professional or technical sphere of the conclusions he has reached on the basis of his knowledge, from facts reported to him or discovered by him by tests, measurements or similar means'. Most doctors providing evidence to courts in child abuse cases are asked to give both professional and expert opinion thereby qualifying for expert fees. For example, the description of injuries encountered during an examination would count as factual (professional) evidence, but further opinion about the causation and level of force required to inflict such injuries would be expert evidence.

The expert witness is a friend of the court. The purpose of his evidence is to furnish the court with specialist information which is likely to be outside the experience and knowledge of a magistrate, judge or jury. The expert witness can read other witnesses' statements and be in court for their evidence, and can comment on both. He can refer to reference books, journals, statistics, as well as his own experience to support his opinion. He is expected to be objective, not selective, in the disclosure of his findings.

The late Leonard Taitz, a paediatrician with much insight, wrote the following:

> Before stepping into the box, the medical expert witness ought to be able to satisfy his or her own conscience on the following questions:
>
> 1.   How expert is he or she, and is that expertise actually relevant to the case being tried?
> 2.   Is he or she an expert in child abuse?
> 3.   Is the claim being put to the court being based on anecdote?
> 4.   Is the experience that he or she is claiming second hand?

5. Is the claim based on a possibly false extrapolation from some other situation?
6. Would the same advice have been proffered to the other side?
7. What are the motives for taking on the case?

An expert should always be cognisant of the boundaries of his expertise. In matters of human nature and behaviour he is no more expert than magistrate, judge or jury.

An important distinction between criminal and civil proceedings is the onus of proof required to satisfy the court. Criminal courts require proof beyond reasonable doubt whereas proof in the Family Court is based on the balance of probability. This fundamental difference enables many children to be protected by removal from their homes where there is insufficient evidence to mount a criminal prosecution.

The usual court procedure follows in this sequence:

1. Opening speech by the applicant/prosecution, who then calls his
2. Evidence in chief. Further questions by judge/magistrate seeking clarification may follow.
3. Cross-examination follows, and then
4. Re-examination by the applicant/prosecutor. Questions arising out of cross-examination are asked taking care not to introduce new topics.
5. This is repeated with each of the applicant/prosecutor's witnesses.
6. The defendant then calls his evidence in the same way.
7. Rebuttal evidence may be called after this.
8. A closing speech is usually made by the defendant only.

The following hints are given to doctors taking the stand in child abuse cases.

1. Be well prepared. Original notes and your statement can be referred to while giving evidence. The importance of legible, detailed notekeeping cannot be overemphasised. Cases come to court many months after the incident and details committed to memory are soon lost. In general it is usually not the injuries themselves that are contested but the cause. It is therefore very important to be able to provide a detailed description of the history provided by the parents at the time of the incident. Under the Children Act 1989 hearsay evidence is acceptable in certain proceedings. If evidence is being provided and your opinion is based on observations by others then these observations should be checked, in any event the court should be made fully aware to what extent your evidence is not first hand. Should the other side call an expert, try to obtain a copy of his statement before the proceedings commence. It is helpful to know in which areas

of the case there is commonality so that these can be discounted and preparation made for areas of contention.

2. Dress smartly and soberly and act with dignity. It is customary to stand and bow to magistrates and judges when they enter and leave the courtroom. Similarly, when you enter or leave a court that is in session a modest bow to the bench or judge is appropriate.

3. Arrive at the court early as counsel may wish to discuss your evidence before proceedings commence. There is frequently a lot of waiting time at the courts and it is worthwhile taking something to read.

4. When giving evidence try not to deviate from the written evidence which has already been given in your statement. Speak loudly, slowly and be concise. Address your evidence to the magistrates, judge or jury and not to counsel asking the questions. Where medical jargon is used it should be explained in plain language, e.g. the child was cyanosed means the child had a blue appearance. Illustrate your points with photographs, x-rays or diagrams. The aphorism that every picture tells a story is a truism in court.

When cross-examined reply with short answers. Use of yes and no answers may require qualification. For example, a three month old with a fractured femur – Question: 'Is it possible to fall and fracture a femur?' Answer: 'Yes, but not at three months.' If the answer is simply 'yes' it will be built on by the advocate in his closing speech. No expert is omniscient. If the answer is not known say 'I don't know' or 'I am not sure'. If a question is not clear do not attempt to answer. Ask for the question to be repeated with further amplification.

Hearsay evidence is not permitted in criminal proceedings. In civil proceedings such evidence given in connection with the upbringing, maintenance or welfare of a child is allowed. This includes cases brought under the Children Act 1989.

During evidence the correct form of address should be used: 'Sir', 'Ma'am', 'Your Worship' (now seldom used) for magistrates; 'Your honour' for Crown and county court judges; 'My Lord', 'My Lady' for High Court judges and all judges at the Central Criminal Court ('Old Bailey').

5. When your evidence is complete ask the court if you can be released.

Prior to giving evidence in court a witness will usually have produced a 'medical' or police report. The solicitor requesting the medical report may ask the doctor to address certain issues. This assists the doctor in that by the questions asked he is able to determine the aspects of the case which will most likely be at issue. The police report is typed on a police statement form which should be provided by the police when the report is requested. Some police officers write the report in the presence of the doctor and ask the doctor to sign it. Should a doctor wish to write the police report in his own time and language he has every right to do so. Police reports written by policemen tend to have police jargon, e.g. a child is referred to as a 'minor'.

Suggestions for writing medical reports are listed below:

1. The typing should be double spaced with wide margins and the pages numbered. Each page should be clearly paragraphed.
2. The document should be headed 'Medical Report' and dated. The child's name and date of birth should be written beneath. It is helpful to include the age of the child as well.
3. Provide your full name, qualifications and post held. Give information about your experience and expertise, e.g. 'I am a community paediatrician of 12 years' standing and have written chapters on child abuse in two textbooks on paediatrics'.
4. State the reason for your involvement, e.g. 'Jackson and Company (solicitors) asked me to provide a medical report'.
5. State the information on which the report is based, e.g. 'My report is based on examination of the casenotes, x-rays and photographs' or 'My report is based on review of the relevant casenotes and medical examination'.
6. Provide general information about the child such as weight, height (including centiles), development and behaviour. Any other relevant information from the past medical history or family history should be included.
7. List specific injuries, their likely age and causation. It may be necessary to refer to photographs, x-rays and coagulation studies. Where medical jargon is used provide an explanation in brackets, e.g. 'extensive ecchymosis (bruising) was noted over the tibia (shin bone)'.
8. List the parental explanation for each injury, if any.
9. Summarise the facts of the case. This may be omitted if the case is not lengthy or complicated.
10. State your conclusion and the reason why you reach that conclusion, e.g. 'A child of three months would not be able to crawl, the bruising on the side of the face could not have been caused by falling down stairs. Furthermore, fingermarks were apparent in the bruising indicating that the child was struck by a hand'. Where possible use concise terms such as accidental or non-accidental. Terms such as 'compatible with' or 'consistent with' are unhelpful in which case further clarification will be sought.

It is most important that a copy of the police statement or medical report be retained. This will assist preparation for subsequent testimony should it be required. There is a standard fee for a police statement. Recommended fees for medical reports can be obtained from the British Medical Association. Under the Children Act 1989 doctors are prohibited from undertaking a medical or psychiatric examination or assessment of a child for the purpose of expert evidence in court proceedings without permission of the court.

There are regulations about the exchange of expert evidence. Section 81 of the Police and Criminal Evidence Act 1984 enables the Crown Court to require either party to disclose to the other any expert evidence adduced in the proceedings. Any such evidence not so disclosed may not be adduced without the consent of the court. In civil cases brought under the Children Act 1989, the party calling a witness must file with the court and serve on other parties a written statement of the oral evidence which the party intends to call at the proceedings. The report of the medical expert witness will be referred to in that statement and copies of the report will usually be attached.

Despite the fact that civil proceedings are intended as inquisitorial rather than adversarial some solicitors still treat the issue in an adversarial fashion. If the expert report is not in the interest of a particular party, the report can be suppressed, and if necessary another expert opinion sought. To circumvent this course of action it is good practice for doctors to insist that the report be made available to all parties as a precondition of their agreement. Provided this condition is agreed a report is not bound by confidentiality and should be disclosed.

Further reading

1. Brent RL. The irresponsible expert witness: a failure of biomedical graduate education and professional accountability. *Pediatrics*. 1982; **70**: 754–62.
2. Meadow R, Mitchels B. *Medical Reports in ABC of Child Abuse* (ed. R Meadow). London: BMJ Publications, 1989: 49–50.
3. Mitchels B, Meadow R. *About Courts in ABC of Child Abuse* (ed. R Meadow). London: BMJ Publications, 1989: 51–4.
4. Carson D. *Professionals and the Courts*. London: Venture Press, 1990.
5. Gee DJ, Mason JK. *The Courts and the Doctor*. Oxford: Oxford Medical Publications, 1990.
6. Taitz L. Child abuse: some myths and shibboleths. *Hospital Update*. 1991; **17**: 400–6.
7. Ludwig S, Barton M. The physician's role in court. In: Ludwig S and Kornberg AE eds. *Child Abuse*. London: Churchill Livingstone, 1992: 441–9.
8. Mitchels B, Prince A. *The Children Act and Medical Practice*. Bristol: Jordan and Sons Limited (Family Law), 1992.
9. Williams C. Expert evidence in cases of child abuse. *Archives of Disease in Childhood* 1993; **68**: 712–4.

19 European legislation
Allan M. Sale

There has been considerable attention paid to child care policy and its related legislation over the last four decades in some of the countries of Europe. This attention and the raising of awareness of children at risk has not taken place in isolation as other major changes continue to develop. Europe has witnessed considerable shifts in its political, economic and social structure.

Amongst all the high GNP per capita regions in the world, Europe is unique.

> In cultural and historical terms, it is extraordinarily heteregeneous, boasting some fifty major nationalities (not all of which enjoys separate statehood) and nearly as many major languages. European economic development has, therefore, proceeded in the face of, and as a constant challenge to, a whole range of cultural and linguistic barriers.[1]

For nearly half a century, following the conclusion of the second world war in 1945, Europe was cut in half by the bipolar politics of East, West confrontation. Whilst the term *iron curtain* may now seem like a piece of quaint cold war rhetoric, it is a fact that normal human and commerical intercourse between Western and Eastern Europe was for several decades, severely hampered.

> Behind the walls and barbed wire, East European countries, all under communist one party rule and mostly under some degree of domination from Moscow, followed the model of the planned, socialist economy, which excluded large scale private ownership of assets on principal, and excluded normal trading relations with other countries.[1]

Following the East European revolution of 1989 and the removing of the many artifical barriers and politically imposed differences that had separated the East and West a much greater opportunity has arisen for communication at all levels and with all interests being shared across otherwise invisible boundaries. In the field of child care legislation there will now be more opportunity for debate and discussion and the sharing of information, knowledge and ideas across the European mass.

In some countries there have been major movements in child care legislation whilst in other countries there has been little if any. Some countries have child care legislation dating back to the start of the twentieth century whilst other countries have no specific legislation in relation to child protection. Some countries are still struggling with the difficulty of not only recognising the behaviour and symptoms of children at risk but also trying to tackle the very real problem of organising effective child care policies and procedures.

The population of each European country varies considerably, with some countries having a child population of just less than one million (Denmark) whilst other countries have in excess of fourteen million children (Germany). There are markedly different economic bases from which each state can finance specific child care policies. This is irrespective of its political *will* to allocate resources.

Within Europe there are countries with exports of high technology, heavy industry and agriculture and countries that rely on tourism for income. There is a clear difference between those countries that are members of the EEC and those that are members of Europe by their geographical position. Some parts of Europe have a shattered infrastructure due to religious hostilities, war, ethnic divide or a combination of all these, where survival from day to day has become a priority. Little time will be available for a detailed and sensitive service to children at risk of abuse. Such brutal realities will need to be recognised when child care policies are considered across Europe as the world sees it today.

The racial, cultural, religious and historical platforms that family life derive from will vary considerably. These variations together with other differences will influence attitude and approach to the problem of child abuse.

The provision of resources by the state for children varies enormously. Different priorities are given to health, social security systems and education. In some states these are directly targeted at vulnerable children and their families. Some have child protection services solely for child abuse and neglect. Others call on the services of the police force, or rely on varying ministries, for example the Ministry of Welfare, Ministry of Health. There is evidence that a number of countries have yet to recognise child abuse as a national phenomenon.

There is a recognition by some states in Europe that the legal power to intervene in child care cases is a crucial and important tool. Legal reforms have grown out of public concern for abused and neglected children. Other states have seen change, if not in law, in attitude, following pioneering work by individuals or small groups of people. The provision of legislation to protect children is changing or has changed in many countries across Europe, especially in the 1970s and 1980s. Each state has the difficult task of balancing the child's safety with that of the family's privacy and security from state interference.

In the United Kingdom, there are differences in the law between

England and Scotland and Northern Ireland (England and Wales are the same).

Any attempt to compare one piece of legislation with another should take account of history and tradition as well as political, economic, social and religious differences between countries.

Another important consideration in child care legislation is professional experience in the content of the application of the law. That experience is of crucial importance in assisting legislators to formulate laws to protect children. Philosophies change, knowledge grows, experience brings forth new considerations highlighting a need for change in the law.

Governments and agencies who administer the legislation also shift their priorities and consequently child protection may be one of competing priorities in a vastly divergent European Society.

In the United Kingdom change has been most visible. In 1988 following over forty public inquiries into child deaths by the government, a pamphlet was introduced called 'Working Together'. This document which has since been updated in 1991 gave guidance to agencies with an interest in child care provision, and recommended close co-operation in what is now frequently called 'child protection work.'

An important factor influencing child care legislation and enabling such legislation to be monitored is the collection of statistics. In some countries there are government statistics on the frequency of legal proceedings initiated for the protection of children. In others there are no government figures, which is not surprising, as those countries may have no legislation specifically aimed at child protection.

Some of the differences between European countries

Some states have child protection services solely for child abuse or neglect, for instance in the United Kingdom there are the Social Service Departments and the NSPCC which have authorised person status under the current 1989 Children Act. In Finland the Child Care Act provides day care provision for children. In 1987 there were 86 000 children in day care provision.[2]

Austria introduced a new 'Youth Welfare Law' on the 1 July 1989 with a statement that 'the wellbeing of a child is considered to be its physical, emotional and moral wellbeing with the corresponding opportunity for development'.[3]

Belgium has a history of legislation to protect children dating back to pre first world war when a piece of legislation was introduced on the 15 May 1912 (a new piece of legislation was introduced on the 8 April 1965). This legislation provided the state with authority to protect children from abuse in certain situations, 'offences committed to children under the age of 16 would be punished most severely'.[4]

Whilst there is a history of legislation to protect children in Belgium, child abuse and neglect are still relatively new concepts.

There is also a documented history in some parts of Europe of children being brutally hurt and killed as far back as the eighteenth century. In Denmark Joav Merrick[5] has drawn our attention to the statistics of the year 1748 in Copenhagan, 'we see that 3 328 persons died, of which 987 were children who died from being beaten or struck to death'. There is also a recorded medical case of child abuse in Denmark which was published in 1827. The article was on an autopsy report on a two year old child called Emma Jacobine, the victim of fatal child abuse. 'Interviews with the stepfather and grandfather and neighbours revealed all the common features of the battered child syndrome' (Merrick[6]).

Portugal is currently witnessing a growth in the public awareness of children's rights yet it has no specific piece of legislation that has been introduced solely for the prevention of child abuse. However, the 'Young Protection Service' introduced on the 27 October 1978 provides in articles 15, 18 and 19, specific measures for the protection of children. This can lead to 'a prohibition or limitation of parental authority when circumstances demand'.[7] There is provision in Portugal to ensure that violence to children can be pursued by the officers of the law only if the violence is committed with 'depravity or self interest'. (Article 153 of the penal code) (Clemete[8]). Much has already been done and much remains to be done. 'The struggle against ill treatment of children must be carried out in a multi-disciplinary way with close co-operation between legal protection and social protection, all professionals must understand and accept this'.[9]

In Norway, Heap[10] has reported there has been no nationwide survey of child abuse and neglect apart from a survey on sexual abuse.

In 1982 the Child Abuse Commission of Norway conducted a retrospective investigation in five selected counties to determine the extent of abuse and serious neglect. On the basis of the data gathered, the Commission estimated an incidence of 490 cases per million inhabitants. (0 to 15 year olds.) Heap reckons that this investigation reflected more the methological limitations of the study than the actual incidence of child abuse and neglect.

There are two laws protecting the child in Norway, the Child Care Act 1953 and the Children Act 1981. The Child Care Act 1953 requires that each Norwegian municipality should have an elected body, *Child Welfare Committee*, with responsibility for prevention methods of work and for intervening in child welfare matters.

The Children Act 1981 saw the introduction of further preventative and supportive measures such as practical and financial assistance, help with housing, counselling and respite care. Weekend fostering and special educational measures such as day care, nursery and kindergarten were included. Supervision Orders are part of that legislation.

There are now opportunities for movement by professionals across some of the countries of Europe, especially within the EEC. It will be in their interest to ask questions (see below) regarding the current legislation in each country. This will ensure that they are appraised of changes in law and policy in each country. It is likely that the legislation in England and Wales will remain constant for some time as it is recent. At the moment changes to Scottish law are set out in a white paper. Changes similar to the Children Act 1989 are proposed in Northern Ireland.

Questions to be asked by a professional moving to a new country

1. What is the current legislation in that country?
2. What part of the legislation is particular to the workers profession or role?
3. What are the likely consequences for the child and family, if the relevant legislation is not known to the professional?
4. What are the potential consequences and *penalties* to the worker if the legislation is not adhered to?
5. Where can the information be found?

The reason for pursuing these simple questions might be best highlighted by the difference between English, Scottish and Northern Irish law.

The law in England and Wales

The law in England and Wales is primarily governed by the Children Act 1989, which came into force on the 14 October 1991 (see Chapter 16). This Act created a new concept of parental responsibility, meaning the duties, rights and authority which a parent has in respect of his or her child. When a child's parents are married, they both have parental responsibilities. When the father is not married to the mother, he does not have parental responsibility simply through being the father, but he may acquire it either by Court Order or by agreement with the mother. The Children Act covers both public and private law. Private law will be concerned with cases where there is a dispute between two parties for example if there is a disagreement following a divorce regarding who should look after the child. In public cases it is usually the Social Services or in some cases the NSPCC who will instigate Care Proceedings when a child is at risk.

The resulting legislation has tried to achieve a finer balance between the state's right to intervene yet to respect family integrity. It has also striven to provide a working arena where delay is kept to a minimum so the child and family are not left in a legal merry go round. The child's ascertainable wishes are considered and the interest of the child should be paramount.

Since the 14 October 1991 when the Act was introduced into practice, there has been much discussion on its positive and negative influences. (See research by Sale A 1993).

It has demonstrated how legislation can fundamentally affect practice. Since the introduction of the Act in October 1991 there has been a decrease in the number of children taken before the court on protection matters. The impact of the new legislation has also changed the attitude of those responsible for implementing child protection plans and procedures in line with the Children Act guidance.

The law in Scotland

There have been many occasions when the results of Public Enquiries following a child death have been at the centre of media attention, in almost all areas of England and Wales.

Scotland has not escaped the attention of the media and the scrutiny of government on the subject of child care practice. The most recent case was the Orkney Inquiry.[11] Lord Clyde produced a 363 page report and it was released in Edinburgh on the 27 October 1992. The report followed widespread concern about the manner nine children were detained by the Orkney Islands Council.

Four families were involved. The children were alleged to be involved in 'Lewd and libidinous practices'[12] and the parents strongly disputed the allegations. The cost of the enquiry is estimated at £6 000 000. It contained 194 recommendations.[13] 'Where reform of the Social Work (Scotland) Act 1968 was necessary to deal better with child protection, Lord Clyde recommended that the amended laws should be reformed so as to be compatible with the European Convention on Human Rights and the UN Convention on the Rights of Child'.

The report was acknowledged for its thoroughness and should be read in full to appreciate its content. The influence of the events in Orkney on the white paper is unclear, also the full scope of the proposals on the reform of child care is uncertain.

The main grounds for child protection work in Scotland can be found in the Social Work (Scotland) Act 1968. Section 32 (2) states the main grounds for taking a child before a formal court setting. These are as follows:

(a) That the child is beyond the control of his parents.
(b) That the child is falling into bad associations or is exposed to moral danger.
(c) That lack of parental care is likely to cause the child unecessary suffering or seriously impair his health or development.

(d) That any of the offences mentioned in schedule 1 of the Criminal Procedure (Scotland) Act 1975 has been committed in respect of the child, or in respect of a child who is a member of the same household.

(e) That the child is presently or is likely to become, a member of the same household as a person who has committed any of the offences mentioned in schedule 1 to the Criminal Procedure (Scotland) Act 1975.

(f) That the child being a female is a member of the same household as a female in respect of whom an offence which constitutes the crime of incest has been committed by a member of that household.

The term *child* is a reference to a boy or girl under the age of 16 years. The second definition of child in the Social Work (Scotland) Act 1968 includes children who are subject to a supervision requirement of a Children's Hearing and could involve children under 18 years.

In Scottish law, nothing has happened unless what is alleged to have occurred can be re-enacted or rehearsed in evidence put before the Sheriff. 'The Sheriff will know nothing about the case before he comes to hear it. He has a completely open mind except that, from the start, the offender or alleged uncaring parent is deemed to be entirely innocent of the allegations unless the contrary is proved'.[14]

When public cases are heard within the context of the Scottish legislation it is important to recognise a number of fundamental principals that those hearing the case will adhere to. Evidence should be told 'how it was'. It is a matter for the court to reach a conclusion whether the objective or 'reasonable man' test has been satisfied, or whether additionally, in cases involving criminal offences against children the behaviour was the product of a *wilful or reckless state of mind*.

In the recent work by the Scottish Child and Family Alliance, *In the Child's Best Interests*,[15] a number of questions are raised.

These are:

1. Who are the parents of a child and in what ways and to what extent is either the parent or any other third party connected to a child, however temporarily, expected by the law to discharge that responsibility and to what extent?

2. At what age does a child cease to be a child for a range of relevant purposes; to what extent and at what age does a child become responsible for himself or herself; how much weight should be given to the child's view of the evidence?

3. What exactly is child abuse'?

4. How is child abuse investigated and what are the organisational structures and processes involved?

5. What can be done to protect children from further abuse and in what circumstances is it not possible to work with the child and

parents on a co-operative and voluntary basis?
6.   What are the rights of parents and children in the face of investi-
     gation and intervention?

Within the Scottish legal framework the relevant sections of the
Social Work (Scotland) Act 1968 have been in force since April 1971
and it defines a system that differs from the arrangements in place
in other parts of the United Kingdom. Central to the operation of
the Scottish system are the activites of nearly 2000 members of
children's panels. The panels are bodies of lay men (both sexes)
recruited locally, where members of the community are invited to
volunteer for this form of unpaid public service. They are selected on
the basis of procedures intended to identify such desirable personal
attributes as open mindedness, ability to communicate and freedom
from extreme degrees of permissiveness or punitiveness. It is also
important to ensure a reasonably balanced representation of age
groups, the sexes and broad social economic categories.[16] 'Three
members of a children's panel constitute a children's hearing and are
responsible for making decisions concerning children who in earlier
times would have been, or are now, in other jurisdictions, dealt with
by juvenile courts or similar bodies. They differ from such forums
however not merely in name but in a number of extremely significant
respects. Cases may reach them only through their Reporter who has
complete freedom to decide whether or not a given child should be
brought before a hearing.'

The panel members, on referral of a case, are not empowered to
debate guilt or innocence. The grounds of referral must be put to
the child and the parents and if they are denied by any of them
the hearing has no further jurisdiction. The matter must then be
referred to a Sheriff for proof, that is to say, for a judicial decision
as to whether the grounds of referral are valid.[17] 'If they are upheld,
the case must be referred back to the hearing for disposal, disposal
means in effect a decision whether a period of supervision by a
social worker is desirable, whether the child should be required to
enter a residential establishment, or whether the referral should be
discharged.' *Martin* goes on to state that a Supervision Order, with
or without a residential requirement, must be reviewed within a year
and may be reviewed at any time if requested by the social worker and
at any time after three months if requested by the child or a parent.
In reaching its decision the hearing is required to take into account
not only the events specified in the statement of grounds but also all
relevent aspects of the child's circumstances. To that end the panel
members will have available, social work and school reports as well
as, on occasion, reports from more specialised agencies.

Above all, panel members are required to make a disposal that is
'in the best interests of the child'.[18]

In Scotland the Sheriff is an experienced legal practitioner who holds a permanent judicial office under the Crown. The Reporter is the official responsible for deciding which matters will come before a hearing. He or she acts as legal advisor to the panel and manages the necessary administration. Any member of the public, concerned for any reason about the welfare of the child, can bring information to the Reporter for his or her consideration.

The law in Northern Ireland

In Northern Ireland the main piece of legislation used in child protection work is the Children and Young Person Act (NI 1968). This legislation has been in force for over 20 years and is soon to be succeeded by a new piece of legislation. There is currently a draft document on the new legislation. It is presently known as: Children (Northern Ireland) Order 1993.

Much of the new proposed legislation mirrors the principals of the Children Act 1989 currently used in England and Wales. There is no date for this new legislation to be brought into force but it is anticipated to be some time in late 1995 or early 1996.

Until this occurs the current Children and Young Person Act (NI 1968) is law. Many of the principals relating to good practice that flow from the Children Act 1989 are already being used in Northern Ireland.

Current similarities between Northern Ireland, England and Wales include:

1. Social workers qualifications are controlled by the central council for education and training in social work.
2. Statutory social workers are employed by an agency similar to the Social Services Department in the UK. In Northern Ireland social services are integrated with social workers and the system is managed by multi-disciplinary general managers.
3. The legislative framework permits a wide range of Protection Orders, e.g. Supervision Orders, Fit Person Orders, etc.

Whilst there are many similarities in the Northern Ireland system to that of England and Wales, the court system does provide for a number of court orders which are nevertheless different.

Child protection work in general enjoys a multi-disciplinary approach and there are many examples of work partnerships between the various statutory and voluntary agencies. Child protection administration arrangements are based upon area Child Protection Committees and each of the four Area Health Authorities.

Social Service Boards publish separate sets of guidelines which reflect a multidisciplinary approach.

In conclusion, it can be seen that there are differences albeit small in some areas between Scotland and England/Wales and to a much lesser degree between England/Wales and Northern Ireland. There are vast differences between the United Kingdom and other parts of Europe. It is the responsibility of the child care professional to seek out and identify the relevant legislation in that part of Europe where he/she works. It is not possible to have a comprehensive list of the various pieces of legislation throughout Europe as they are too numerous and the constant change would soon render them obsolete.

References

1. Dyker D. *The European Economy*. London: Longman, 1992.
2. Kivinen T. *Prevention and Protection in Europe*, eds Davies M, Sale A, London: NSPCC, 1989.
3. Paulischin H. Child Protection Policies and Practice in Europe. In *Austrian Dimension*, eds Sale A, Davies M. London: NSPCC, 1990.
4. Marneffe C. *Prevention and Protection in Europe*, Sale A, Davies M, 1989.
5. Merrick J. Danish Society for the Prevention of Child Abuse and Neglect. In: *Child Protection Policies and Practice in Europe*, eds Sale A, Davies M, 1990.
6. Merrick J. Danish Society for Abuse and Neglect. In: *Child Protection Policies and Practice in Europe*, eds Sale A, Davies M, 1990.
7. Clemente RM. Portugal Dimension. In: *Prevention and Protection in Europe*, eds Davies M, Sale A, 1989.
8. Clemente RM. Portugal Dimension. In: *Prevention and Protection in Europe*, eds Davies M, Sale A, 1989.
9. Clemente RM. Portugal Dimension. In: *Prevention and Protection in Europe*, eds Davies M, Sale A, 1989.
10. Heap KK. Norwegian Institute of Child Welfare Research, 1990.
11. Bissett-Johnstone A. The Orkney Report. Key issues for lawyers. In: *Journal of Child Care Law*, Vol 5, No. 2, 1993.
12. Bissett-Johnstone A. The Orkney Report. Key issues for lawyers. In: *Journal of Child Care Law*, Vol 5, No. 2, 1993.
13. Bissett-Johnstone A. The Orkney Report. Key issues for lawyers. In: *Journal of Child Care Law*, Vol 5, No. 2, 1993.
14. Scottish Child and Family Alliances. *In the Child's Best Interests*. Crown Copyright, 1991. ISBN 011 4941327.
15. Scottish Child and Family Alliances. *In the Child's Best Interests*. Crown Copyright, 1991. ISBN 011 4941327.
16. Martin FM, Murray K, Millar H. *The Role of "Children's Hearings" in Child Abuse and Neglect. Pergamon Press*. 1982.
17. Martin FM, Murray K, Millar H. *The Role of "Children's Hearings" in Child Abuse and Neglect. Pergamon Press*. 1982.
18. Martin FM, Murray K, Millar H. *The Role of "Children's Hearings" in Child Abuse and Neglect. Pergamon Press*. 1982.

Index